Hey, Leslie! What's Cooking?

Leslie Bailey

*Dearest Susan,
Thank-you for being one
of the kindest people I've
ever met! I am blessed to
have you as a friend!
Fondly,
Leslie*

RCP

RIVER CITY PUBLISHING
MONTGOMERY, ALABAMA

Published in the United States by River City Publishing
1719 Mulberry St.
Montgomery, AL 36106.

Designed by Lissa Monroe
Photographs by Russ Baxley

First Edition—2004
Printed in the United States of America
1   3   5   7   9   10   8   6   4   2

Library of Congress Cataloging-in-Publication Data

Bailey, Leslie (Leslie M.), 1954-
Hey, Leslie! What's cooking? / by Leslie Bailey.-- 1st ed.
p. cm.
ISBN 1-57966-053-3
1. Cookery. I. Title.
TX714.B3334 2004
641.5--dc22

2004010057

This cookbook is dedicated to the unsung heroes of Hospice of Montgomery, who taught me that even in Death there is Life. And to my mom, Bobbye Jane Middlebrooks Morris, whose heart is still beating in the woman I have become.

TABLE OF CONTENTS

I wrote this cookbook for everyone who is tired of trying to find yak milk from the mountains of Nepal or can't make a soufflé for all the tea in China. My recipes are easy to follow and never, never, never require hard-to-find ingredients. And, for that matter, they never require a lot of time to complete.

I have designated myself a "real person's Martha Stewart." Okay, okay, so I don't have my own line of cookware or linens or bakeware . . . who cares! I have a fantastic group of recipes that will make you shine and allow you to be the domestic diva you've always wanted to be.

Some of the recipes in this book are ones that I used in the Silver Spoon Café and still use in my catering business. People ask for these recipes a lot, and now you'll have them! You can tell which ones are the Silver Spoon signature recipes because they have the Silver Spoon logo next to the recipe title. I hope you enjoy making and eating them as much as I do!

Also, some of the recipes in this book will work just fine with margarine instead of butter or with low-fat/low-sugar ingredients. But others require the flavor or cooking properties of the butter or the regular ingredients. If the recipe doesn't mention margarine or low-fat/low-sugar ingredients, the finished product won't turn out right if you try to use substitutes for the "real" thing.

I hope you always have a delicious day!

Leslie Bailey

Clockwise from top: Black-Eyed Pea Dip, Fruit Kabobs with Honey-Banana Cream, Raspberry-Cheddar Mold

Appetizers

In Rogers and Hammerstein's eternally popular show, *The Sound of Music*, the governess, Maria, sings, "Let's start at the very beginning, a very good place to start!"

Well, if these words are good enough for Fraulein Maria, then they're good enough for me. So this chapter will be about beginnings—appetizers (or, as the snooty like to call them, "hors d'oeuvres").

These appetizers, in my opinion, are "perfect in every way" (a phrase made famous by another governess, Miss Mary Poppins). They're easy, they're quick, and they'll have your crowd shouting for encores.

In the musical *Camelot*, Guinevere sings, "What else do the simple folk do?" Well, let me say this: We simple folk have plenty else to do besides spending tedious hours in the kitchen slaving over party appetizers. We do, after all, have lives to live.

So you have my guarantee: These tasty starters are simple—and they're simply fabulous!

Fruit Kabobs with Honey-Banana Cream

You can use any combination of your favorite fruits. Let your kids help arrange the kabobs—it's a great way to get them to eat more fruit!

1	cup mashed banana
1	cup powdered sugar
1	cup sour cream
1	teaspoon ground cinnamon
24	strawberries
24	banana chunks
24	red or green seedless grapes
24	cantaloupe chunks
	Chopped pecans (optional)

Combine first 4 ingredients in a bowl, stirring well. Cover and chill.

Arrange fruit on 12 (12-inch) wooden skewers, placing 8 pieces of fruit on each skewer.

Sprinkle chopped pecans on honey-banana cream, if desired, and serve with fruit kabobs.

Yield: 12 servings

You can use low-fat sour cream to make this even healthier, too!

Fudge-aholic Fruit Dip

I like to serve this dip with vanilla wafers because then it seems more like dessert! But if you insist on being healthy, serve it with strawberries or apple and pear slices. Plus, the fruit adds some color if you're serving it at a party.

⅓	cup fat-free hot fudge topping
⅓	cup fat-free vanilla yogurt
1½	teaspoons orange juice

Combine all ingredients in a bowl. Cover and chill at least 30 minutes. Serve with vanilla wafers or fresh fruit.

Yield: 6 servings

Cranberry Cream Cheese

Be sure to use the whole-berry type of canned cranberry sauce, not the jellied kind.

1	(16-ounce) can whole-berry cranberry sauce
½	cup apricot preserves
⅓	cup slivered almonds, toasted
2	tablespoons lemon juice
1	(8-ounce) package cream cheese

Combine first 4 ingredients in a bowl, stirring well. Spoon cranberry mixture over cream cheese; serve with crackers.

Yield: 6 to 8 servings

You can use low-fat or no-fat cream cheese in this, if you like!

Feta Delight

If you've got "low-carbers" coming to your party, this yummy cheese dish is what you need. Leave off the French bread and serve it with fresh veggies or fried pork skins.

1	(8-ounce) block feta cheese
1	large red or green bell pepper, cut into 4 to 6 rings
1	large purple onion, cut into 8 rings
¼	cup olive oil
	Salt (optional)
	Pepper (optional)
2	tablespoons chopped fresh rosemary, basil, or oregano
	French bread slices, toasted

Preheat oven to 350°F.

Slice feta cheese into strips; place on large sheet of aluminium foil. Top cheese with pepper rings and onion slices.

Drizzle olive oil over cheese and vegetables; sprinkle with salt and pepper, if desired. Sprinkle fresh herbs over cheese and vegetables.

Fold foil over cheese, sealing to make a packet. Bake at 350°F for 10 to 15 minutes or until cheese melts. Remove from foil; serve with toasted French bread slices.

Yield: 8 servings

Garlic-Dill Crostini with Italian Tomato Chutney

"Crostini" is just a fancy word for little slices of French bread. This is definitely an appetizer that will impress your "hoity toity" friends.

4	ripe tomatoes, chopped
1	(2¼-ounce) can chopped black olives, drained
3	scallions, chopped
1	tablespoon minced garlic
3	tablespoons olive oil
¼	teaspoon coarse salt
	Pinch of chopped cilantro
1	French bread baguette
½	stick butter or margarine, melted
¼	teaspoon garlic salt
¼	teaspoon dried dill

Preheat oven to 300°F.

Combine first 7 ingredients, stirring well.

To make crostini, cut baguette into 24 thin slices. Brush with melted butter; sprinkle with garlic salt and dill. Bake at 300°F until lightly toasted.

To serve, top bread slices evenly with tomato mixture.

Yield: 2 dozen appetizers

Watermelon Salsa

This fruit salsa doesn't have any fat, so it's really good for you. If you're trying to lose weight for your class reunion or to fit into a new swimsuit, serve it with low-fat tortilla chips.

6	cups diced, seeded watermelon, drained
1	cup chopped green bell pepper
6	tablespoons fresh lime juice (about 3 limes)
2	tablespoons chopped fresh basil
6	scallions, chopped
¼	cup chopped jalapeño pepper
1	teaspoon minced garlic

Combine all ingredients in a large bowl, stirring well. Cover and chill.

Serve with tortilla chips.

Yield: 6 servings

Shrimp Salsa on Cheese

This is a sassy low-carb dip. For crunch, serve it with fried pork skins instead of tortilla chips.

2	pounds small salad shrimp
1	cup fresh chopped tomato
2	tablespoons fresh lime juice (about 1 lime)
2	garlic cloves
1	(15-ounce) jar mild chunky salsa
1	onion, finely chopped
1	(8-ounce) package cream cheese

Combine first 6 ingredients, stirring well.

Cover and chill overnight.

To serve, spoon shrimp mixture over cream cheese. Serve with tortilla chips.

Yield: 8 servings

For an even healthier version, use low-fat or no-fat cream cheese.

Black-Eyed Pea Dip

We "belles" call this "Southern caviar."

1	(15.8-ounce) can black-eyed peas, rinsed and drained
1	(15-ounce) can whole-kernel corn, drained
1	(10-ounce) can diced tomatoes and green chilies (such as Rotel), drained
1	cup chopped green bell pepper
¾	cup Italian dressing
2	scallions, chopped
1	teaspoon chopped cilantro

Combine all ingredients, stirring well. Cover and chill.

Serve with tortilla chips or corn chips.

Yield: 8 to 12 servings

Reduced-calorie dressing helps us keep our "belle" figures!

Bacon-and-Corn Dip

You can make this reduced-fat dip by using the low-fat versions of cream cheese, sour cream, and mayonnaise. And, if you're really hard core, you can use turkey bacon and serve it with reduced-fat crackers instead of Fritos.

1	(8-ounce) package cream cheese, softened
1	cup sour cream
¼	cup mayonnaise
2	garlic cloves, minced
1	teaspoon hot pepper sauce
1	(11-ounce) can whole-kernel corn, drained
8	bacon slices, cooked and crumbled

Combine first 5 ingredients, stirring well. Stir in corn and bacon. Cover and chill at least 2 hours.

Serve with corn chips or crackers.

Yield: 8 servings

Horseradish-Shrimp Dip with Sautéed Almonds

If you shop at a supermarket with a seafood department, just run in and ask for about ½ pound of cooked shrimp. If you want to cook it yourself, you'll need about ¾ pound unpeeled shrimp to get 8 ounces of cooked shrimp.

1	cup slivered almonds
3	tablespoons butter or margarine
1	(8-ounce) package cream cheese, softened
1	cup chopped cooked shrimp (6 to 8 ounces)
3	tablespoons picante sauce
2	tablespoons prepared horseradish
1	teaspoon garlic salt

Heat butter in a medium skillet. Add almonds and sauté until lightly browned. Drain and set almonds aside.

Combine cream cheese and next 4 ingredients. Place cheese mixture in a serving dish and sprinkle with almonds.

Serve with crackers.

Yield: 8 servings

Use low-fat or no-fat cream cheese for fewer calories!

Shrimp Dip

This creamy dip is easy to throw together if you've got unexpected company.

1	(16-ounce) carton sour cream
2	(4¼-ounce) cans tiny shrimp, rinsed in cold water and drained
¼	cup finely chopped scallions
2	tablespoons ketchup
1	tablespoon prepared horseradish

Combine all ingredients, stirring well. Cover and chill.

Serve with corn chips or crackers.

Yield: 8 to 10 servings

Using low-fat or no-fat sour cream will help out anyone on a diet!

Zesty Hummus with Pita Wedges

This Middle Eastern-style spread will wow your friends. And it couldn't be any quicker!

1	(15½-ounce) can garbanzo beans, drained
1	cup mayonnaise
1	red bell pepper, chopped
1	green bell pepper, chopped
½	cup minced onion
2	tablespoons Italian dressing
1	teaspoon dried oregano
1	teaspoon sesame seeds
1	teaspoon minced garlic
3	teaspoons lemon juice
6	pita bread rounds

Combine all ingredients except pita bread in a food processor; process until smooth.

Cut each pita round into 4 wedges; serve with hummus.

Yield: 12 servings

Ham Spread

This is a great way to use up all that ham you have left over from the holidays.

2	cups diced cooked ham
2	tablespoons canned artichoke hearts, drained and chopped
2	tablespoons chopped onion
2	tablespoons mayonnaise (add more, if desired)
2	tablespoons sour cream
1	tablespoon Creole mustard

Combine all ingredients. Cover and chill. Serve with crackers or corn chips.

Yield: 6 to 8 servings

Ballgame Beer-Cheese Spread

Serve this cheesy dip with your favorite cracker—I think it's really yummy on Wheat Thins.

2	cups (8 ounces) finely shredded sharp Cheddar cheese
1	cup beer
3	tablespoons tomato sauce
2	teaspoons Worcestershire sauce
1	teaspoon garlic salt

Combine all ingredients, beating with a mixer.

Serve with crackers.

Yield: 8 to 10 servings

Sweet Onion-Cheese Spread

When they're available, I love to use Vidalia onions for this hot spread.

2	tablespoons butter or margarine
3	large sweet onions, coarsely chopped
1	garlic clove, minced
2	cups (8 ounces) shredded sharp Cheddar cheese
1	cup mayonnaise
½	teaspoon hot pepper sauce

Preheat oven to 375°F.

Melt butter in a large skillet. Add onions and garlic; sauté until tender.

Remove from heat; stir in cheese, mayonnaise, and hot pepper sauce.

Spoon into an 11 x 7-inch baking dish. Bake at 375°F for 18 to 25 minutes or until lightly browned and bubbly.

Serve with crackers.

Yield: 8 servings

Pecan-Pimiento Cheese

You asked for it . . . and here it is! This was one of the most popular items on the Silver Spoon Café's menu, and we made vats of it. This is a more manageable amount for your family.

2	cups (8 ounces) shredded extra-sharp Cheddar cheese
2	cups (8 ounces) shredded sharp Cheddar cheese
1½	cups mayonnaise (add more, if desired)
½	cup chopped pecans
½	cup chopped black olives
1	(4-ounce) jar diced pimiento, drained and patted very dry

Combine all ingredients; stir well. Cover and chill.

Serve with crackers or in small sandwiches.

Yield: 10 to 12 servings

Saucy Ham-and-Cheese Dip

This combination of sweet and salty is irresistible.

2	(8-ounce) packages cream cheese, softened
2	(4-ounce) cans deviled ham spread
¼	teaspoon ground red pepper (cayenne)
1	(8-ounce) can crushed pineapple, well drained
⅓	cup chopped scallions

Combine cream cheese, ham, and pepper in large bowl. Beat with a mixer until smooth.

Add pineapple and scallions; stir well. Cover and chill 30 minutes.

Serve with crackers or cocktail bread.

Yield: 8 servings

Using low-fat/no-fat cream cheese means this recipe is healthier, too!

Chocolate Chip-Cheese Ball

I often roll the ball in mini-chocolate chips and put it on my dessert table. Everybody loves this!

1	(8-ounce) package cream cheese
1	cup mini-chocolate chips
½	cup powdered sugar
¼	cup butter or margarine, softened
½	teaspoon vanilla extract
1	cup chopped pecans

Combine first 5 ingredients, stirring well.

Shape mixture into a ball; roll ball in pecans. Cover and chill.

Serve with graham crackers, gingersnaps, or vanilla wafers.

Yield: 8 to 10 servings

Mexican Cheese Ball

Ole'! A south-of-the-border cheese appetizer that's perfect for Cinco de Mayo parties.

⅔	cup chopped pecans
1	tablespoon butter or margarine, melted
⅛	teaspoon salt
2	(8-ounce) packages cream cheese, softened
1½	cups (6 ounces) shredded Cheddar cheese
½	cup picante sauce
6	tablespoons taco seasoning
4	scallions, chopped

Combine pecans, melted butter, and salt; stir well to coat pecans. Place pecans in a small baking dish, and bake at 350°F for 4 to 5 minutes or until toasted. Set aside to cool.

Combine cream cheese and next 4 ingredients, stirring well. Shape mixture into a ball. Roll cheese ball in toasted pecans, coating well. Cover and chill until ready to serve.

Serve with assorted crackers.

Yield: 16 servings

Triple Cheese Ball

This is the cheese ball I do for holiday parties because of the festive red and green of the peppers.

2	(8-ounce) packages cream cheese, softened
1	cup (4 ounces) shredded Cheddar cheese
¼	cup (1 ounce) crumbled blue cheese
½	cup chopped red bell pepper
½	cup chopped green bell pepper
¼	cup chopped scallions
½	teaspoon garlic salt
½	teaspoon dried dill
	Paprika

Combine all ingredients, stirring well. Shape mixture into a ball. Cover and chill overnight.

Roll cheese ball in paprika, coating heavily. Serve with assorted crackers.

You can make bite-sized cheese balls and insert a pretzel stick before serving. Instant cheese "lollipops"!

Yield: 16 servings

"Apple" Cheese Ball

Present this to your teacher and you're sure to get an A+!

2	cups (8 ounces) shredded Cheddar cheese
1	(8-ounce) package cream cheese, softened
1	teaspoon garlic powder
⅛	teaspoon ground red pepper
	Paprika
1	(3-inch) cinnamon stick
1	bay leaf

Combine first 4 ingredients in a food processor; process until smooth. Cover and chill 30 minutes.

Shape cheese mixture into a ball; make an indentation in the top to resemble the stem end of an apple. Cover and chill 30 minutes.

Coat cheese ball heavily in paprika; insert cinnamon stick and bay leaf to resemble an apple's stem and leaf. Cover and chill at least 1 hour before serving.

Serve with crackers.

Yield: 8 to 10 servings

 ## Raspberry-Cheddar Mold

Any flavor of jam will work in this recipe. I like to use strawberry and blackberry for a change.

4	cups (16 ounces) shredded sharp Cheddar cheese
1	cup pecan pieces
1	cup mayonnaise
1	bunch scallions, chopped
½	teaspoon garlic salt
1	cup raspberry jam

Combine cheese, pecans, mayonnaise, scallions, and garlic salt. (If mixture needs to be creamier, add ¼ to ½ cup more mayonnaise.)

Shape mixture into a ball, pressing in the top to form a well. Spoon raspberry jam into the well. Or, form cheese mixture into star or heart shapes, if desired.

Serve with crackers.

Yield: 8 servings

Party Brie

You can never go wrong with Brie. This one is to die for because of the Parmesan, sun-dried tomatoes, and walnuts that you sprinkle on top. It might be a good idea to do two of these because one will go fast!

⅓	cup chopped fresh parsley
2	tablespoons chopped fresh basil
3	tablespoons olive oil
12	garlic cloves, minced
10	sun-dried tomatoes in oil, drained and chopped
1	(16-ounce) round Brie cheese
⅓	cup shredded fresh Parmesan cheese
3	tablespoons chopped walnuts

Combine first 5 ingredients, stirring well. Cut top rind off of Brie; place the Brie on a serving plate. Score with a knife. Top with herb mixture; sprinkle Parmesan cheese and walnuts over herb mixture.

Let stand at room temperature for 2 hours before serving.

Serve with crackers.

Yield: 8 servings

Kickoff Kabobs

Depending on the length of your wooden skewers, you should be able to make about 12 kabobs. If you fill up 12 skewers and still have ingredients left, just make some more. It's always good to have a few extra to nibble on.

1	(9-ounce) package refrigerated cheese tortellini
1	(14-ounce) can artichoke hearts, drained and quartered
1	(2¼-ounce) can pitted ripe olives, drained
1	(12-ounce) package pepperoni slices
8	ounces cubed mozzarella or Cheddar cheese
1	pint cherry tomatoes
1	(8-ounce) bottle Italian dressing

Prepare tortellini according to package directions. Drain.

Alternate tortellini, artichoke hearts, olives, pepperoni slices, cheese cubes, and tomatoes on 12 wooden skewers.

Place kabobs in a large baking dish; pour dressing over kabobs. Cover and chill at least 8 hours.

Remove from dressing; serve at room temperature.

Yield: 1 dozen appetizers

Spinach Rollups

These would make Popeye proud.

1	(10-ounce) package frozen chopped spinach, thawed and squeezed very dry
1	cup mayonnaise
1	(8-ounce) carton sour cream
1	bunch scallions, chopped
1	envelope ranch dressing mix
1	(4.1-ounce) jar bacon bits
9	(10-inch) flour tortillas

Combine first 6 ingredients, stirring well. Spread spinach mixture evenly on tortillas.

Roll up each tortilla, jellyroll style, pressing edges to seal. Wrap each rollup tightly in plastic wrap; chill 4 to 6 hours.

To serve, remove plastic wrap and cut each rollup into 8 slices.

Yield: 6 dozen

Using low-fat sour cream and mayonnaise would make your mama proud!

Taco Pinwheels

These bite-sized treats disappear quickly—you might want to double the recipe.

1	pound ground beef
1	(1¼-ounce) envelope taco seasoning mix
½	(8-ounce) package cream cheese, softened
1	cup (4 ounces) shredded Cheddar cheese
1	cup salsa
2	tablespoons mayonnaise
2	tablespoons chopped ripe olives
2	tablespoons finely chopped onions
5	(6-inch) flour tortillas
1	cup shredded lettuce

Brown ground beef in a skillet, stirring to crumble meat. Drain; stir in taco seasoning mix.

Combine cream cheese, Cheddar cheese, salsa, mayonnaise, olives, and onions. Add cheese mixture to meat, stirring well.

Spread cheese-meat mixture evenly over tortillas; sprinkle with lettuce.

Roll up tortillas tightly, jellyroll style; wrap each roll tightly in plastic wrap.

Cover and chill for at least 1 hour or overnight.

To serve, remove plastic wrap and cut each roll into 5 slices. Serve warm or at room temperature. To serve warm, cover with damp paper towel and microwave for 15-25 seconds.

Yield: 25 pinwheels

And they'll go just as fast if you use low-fat ingredients!

Stuffed Mushroom Caps

Use the largest mushrooms you can find (but not the very large portobellos) to make the mushroom caps.

1	(10-ounce) package frozen chopped spinach, thawed and squeezed very dry
1	cup (4 ounces) crumbled feta cheese
1	cup mayonnaise
½	cup finely chopped onion
½	cup coarsely chopped walnuts
	Dash of salt
	Dash of pepper
	Dash of ground nutmeg
36	large mushroom caps

Preheat oven to 350°F.

Combine spinach, cheese, mayonnaise, onion, and walnuts, stirring well. Add salt, pepper, and nutmeg; stir well.

Place mushroom caps on lightly greased baking sheets. Spoon spinach mixture into mushroom caps, using about 1 tablespoon per cap.

Bake at 350°F for 20 minutes or until lightly browned. Serve warm.

Yield: 3 dozen

Low-fat mayonnaise works great in this recipe!

Spinach Balls

Here's one way to get your kids to eat their spinach. If you know of another way, let me know.

2	(10-ounce) packages frozen chopped spinach, thawed and squeezed very dry
1	pound ground pork sausage
1	(16-ounce) package herbed stuffing mix
1	cup (4 ounces) shredded mozzarella cheese
1	cup (4 ounces) shredded Cheddar cheese
½	cup grated Parmesan cheese
6	eggs
1	large onion, chopped
1	garlic clove, minced

Preheat oven to 350°F.

Crumble raw sausage. Add spinach and remaining ingredients; stir well. Shape mixture into 1-inch balls; place 1 inch apart on a baking sheet.

Bake at 350°F for 20 to 22 minutes or until lightly browned. (You can freeze uncooked spinach balls until you're ready to bake them.)

Yield: 5 dozen

Hot and Cheesy Spinach Appetizers

This dip is lickity-delicious!

1	(8-ounce) package cream cheese, softened
1	(10-ounce) package frozen creamed spinach, thawed
2	cups (8 ounces) shredded Swiss cheese
1	teaspoon garlic salt
1	(16-ounce) loaf French bread

Preheat oven to 350°F.

Combine cream cheese and creamed spinach in a medium-sized bowl. Beat with a mixer at medium speed until smooth. Add cheese and garlic salt, beating well.

Cut a lengthwise wedge (about 1 inch deep) out of the top of the bread and discard. Spoon spinach mixture into opening.

Wrap bread securely in foil. Bake at 350°F for 10 minutes or until hot and bubbly.

Cut into slices and serve warm.

Yield: 6 to 8 servings

To make it healthier, use light cream cheese and reduced-fat Swiss cheese. And it works fine with whole wheat French bread, too!

Hot Artichoke-and-Spinach Dip

Who needs the Fritos? I could just eat this up with a spoon!

1	cup (4 ounces) shredded Cheddar cheese
1	cup grated Parmesan cheese
1	cup mayonnaise
1	(14-ounce) can artichoke hearts, drained and chopped
1	(10-ounce) package frozen chopped spinach, thawed and squeezed very dry
1	garlic clove, minced
	Pinch of nutmeg

Preheat oven to 350°F.

Combine all ingredients in a bowl.

Spoon mixture into a 1½-quart casserole dish; bake at 350°F for 45 minutes.

Serve warm with crackers or corn chips.

Yield: 6 to 8 servings

And it's low-carb friendly; just use pork rinds for scooping!

Shrimpalicious Hot Dip

This fancy dip is always the first to go when I serve it at parties!

1	stick butter or margarine
1	bunch scallions, minced
½	cup whipping cream
2	tablespoons all-purpose flour
3	cups chopped cooked shrimp
2	cups (8 ounces) shredded Swiss cheese
¼	cup minced fresh parsley
1	tablespoon dry cooking sherry
¼	teaspoon garlic salt
	Dash of hot sauce
	Dash of Worcestershire sauce

Preheat oven to 350°F.

Melt butter in a large skillet over medium-high heat. Add scallions; sauté until tender. Remove from heat.

In a bowl, combine whipping cream and flour, stirring well. Add cream mixture to sautéed scallions, stirring well.

Combine shrimp and next 6 ingredients; stir into scallion mixture. Place mixture in a 1½-quart baking dish. Bake at 350°F for 25 to 35 minutes or until hot and bubbly.

Serve warm with crackers.

Yield: 20 servings

Cheesy Artichoke Squares

This treat is basically hot artichoke dip on a crescent roll base. Hard to resist!

2	(8-ounce) cans refrigerated crescent dinner rolls
1	cup (4 ounces) shredded mozzarella cheese
1	cup grated Parmesan cheese
1	cup mayonnaise
1	(15-ounce) can artichoke hearts, drained and finely chopped
1	(4-ounce) can chopped green chilies
½	teaspoon salt
1	red bell pepper, cut into strips (optional)

Preheat oven to 375°F.

Unroll dough; press into 15 x 10-inch baking pan.

Combine mozzarella cheese and next 5 ingredients, stirring well. Spoon mixture onto dough, spreading to cover dough.

Bake at 375°F for 15 minutes or until cheese melts. Let stand 5 minutes; cut into 15 squares. Garnish with red pepper strips, if desired. Serve warm or at room temperature.

Yield: 15 appetizers

Cheesy Sausage Balls

When I know that there will be a bunch of men at a party, I always add sausage balls to the menu. Of course, the women have been known to scarf down a few of these themselves.

2½	cups cheese-garlic or regular biscuit mix (such as Bisquick)
2	cups (8 ounces) shredded Cheddar cheese
½	cup chopped onion
1	pound ground pork sausage

Preheat oven to 350°F.

Combine all ingredients, stirring well. Shape mixture into 1-inch balls and place 1 inch apart on a baking sheet.

Bake at 350°F for 15 to 18 minutes or until lightly browned.

Serve warm.

Yield: 3 dozen

Bacon-Tomato-Cheese Wraps

You may get more than 18 slices of bacon in a 1-pound package; if you do, just cook it up and eat it! Or make more of these tasty little snacks because you'll also have more than 36 crackers in a box. You can't go wrong with anything wrapped in bacon!

18	slices bacon
36	rectangular buttery crackers (such as Waverly Wafers)
1	cup (4 ounces) shredded Cheddar cheese
1	cup chopped Roma tomatoes
	Cooking spray

Preheat oven to 350°F.

Slice each bacon strip in half, crosswise. Wrap 1 strip bacon around each cracker, beginning and ending on backside of cracker.

Place crackers on rack of a broiler pan coated with cooking spray. Bake at 350°F for 35 to 45 minutes or until bacon is done.

Top with shredded cheese and chopped tomatoes and return to oven for 3 to 5 minutes or until cheese melts.

Yield: 3 dozen

Pepperoni-and-Cheese Crescents

These are sort of like mini-pizzas but so much easier to pop into your mouth!

1	(8-ounce) can refrigerated crescent rolls
24	slices pepperoni
1	cup (4 ounces) shredded mozzarella cheese
1	egg, lightly beaten

Preheat oven to 375°F.

Separate crescent roll dough into triangles; place triangles on a baking sheet.

Place 3 slices of pepperoni in each triangle. Sprinkle triangles evenly with mozzarella cheese.

Roll up triangles and curve them into half-moon shapes. Brush with beaten egg. Bake at 375°F for 8 to 10 minutes or until lightly browned.

Yield: 8 servings

Seafood Nacho Supreme

You can use frozen shrimp for these cheesy nachos, but if you're vacationing at the beach, of course you should use fresh!

1	cup (6 ounces) chopped cooked shrimp
1	cup sour cream
½	cup mayonnaise
2	tablespoons finely chopped onion
½	teaspoon chopped fresh dill
30	tortilla chips
1	cup (4 ounces) shredded Cheddar cheese
½	cup sliced black olives
	Paprika

Preheat oven to 350°F.

Combine first 5 ingredients, stirring well.

Place tortilla chips on a large, lightly greased baking sheet. Spoon shrimp mixture evenly onto tortilla chips. Top evenly with Cheddar cheese and olives; sprinkle with paprika.

Bake at 350°F for 8 to 10 minutes or until hot and bubbly.

Yield: 12 servings

If you're worried about fat, use fat-free sour cream, light mayonnaise, and reduced-fat cheese.

Sesame Chicken Strips

These are crispy and yummy and a nice change from rubbery frozen chicken fingers.

1½	cups mayonnaise, divided
2	teaspoons dried minced onion
2	teaspoons dry mustard
1	cup crushed round buttery crackers (such as Ritz)
¼	cup sesame seeds
2	pounds skinless, boneless chicken breasts
½	cup mustard
¼	cup honey

Preheat oven to 425°F.

Combine 1 cup mayonnaise, minced onion, and dry mustard, stirring well.

In a separate bowl, combine crushed crackers and sesame seeds.

Cut chicken into 1-inch-wide strips. Dip chicken strips in mayonnaise mixture and then in cracker mixture, coating well. Place coated chicken strips on a greased baking sheet. Bake at 425°F for 15 minutes or until golden brown.

Combine remaining mayonnaise, mustard, and honey for dipping sauce.

Serve chicken with honey-mustard sauce.

Yield: 12 servings

Notes

Gazpacho

Salads and Soups

If you think that a salad is just a pile of green stuff and that soup is something you heat up from a can when you don't have anything else to eat, you need to revamp your thinking.

For starters, my Silver Spoon signature chicken salad (page 72) doesn't have one bit of green—and I can guarantee it's one of the best salads you'll ever put in your mouth. I'm always getting asked for this recipe. And the pasta salads—which do, occasionally, have a few veggies stirred in—are everybody's favorite at covered-dish suppers.

Soup, to me, is the ultimate comfort food. There's nothing a like a big bowl of cheesy potato soup when you're feeling down. Of course, you have to do a bit more than open up a can, but not much.

So, when you're needing a little simplicity in your life, go for the salad and soup option. Why make things more complicated than they need to be?

Sour Cream-Fruit Salad

There's just nothing better than a "drain and dump" fruit salad.

1	cup pineapple chunks, drained
1	cup sour cream
1	cup mandarin oranges, drained
1	cup mini-marshmallows
1	(11-ounce) can flaked coconut
1	(8-ounce) jar maraschino cherries, drained and chopped
1	cup chopped pecans

Combine first 6 ingredients, stirring well.

Just before serving, sprinkle with chopped pecans.

Yield: 6 servings

Using low-fat or no-fat sour cream cuts the fat and saves some calories!

Pineapple-and-Banana Slaw

Why eat plain ol' coleslaw when you can have this fruity, sweet version?

1	(8-ounce) can pineapple tidbits
3	cups shredded coleslaw mix (without dressing packet)
½	cup mayonnaise
¼	cup sour cream
1	tablespoon honey
1	cup chopped pecans
1	small banana

Drain pineapple, reserving 3 tablespoons juice. Combine coleslaw mix and drained pineapple.

In a separate bowl, combine mayonnaise, sour cream, honey, and reserved pineapple juice, stirring well.

Add mayonnaise mixture to coleslaw mixture, stirring well. Sprinkle with pecans.

Just before serving, slice banana and stir it into mixture.

Yield: 4 to 6 servings

Low-fat mayonnaise and sour cream taste just as good in this, too!

Asparagus Salad with Champagne-Saffron Vinaigrette

I like to make this elegant salad when I'm trying to impress my guests. Even if they don't like it, I've still got that bottle of champagne . . .

1½	pounds asparagus
1	teaspoon saffron threads
1	teaspoon boiling water
½	cup champagne
2	teaspoons Dijon mustard
	Pinch of sugar
3	tablespoons extra-virgin olive oil
½	cup diced red or yellow bell pepper
½	teaspoon salt
¼	teaspoon pepper
	Lettuce leaves

Snap off woody ends of asparagus stalks. Cook asparagus, covered, in a small amount of boiling water 6 to 8 minutes or until crisp-tender. Drain and run under cold water until cooled; drain well.

Stir saffron into 1 teaspoon boiling water; let stand for 2 minutes. Stir in champagne, mustard, and sugar. Add olive oil, salt, and pepper; stir well.

Combine asparagus and diced pepper in a large bowl. Add oil mixture; toss to coat well. Arrange on lettuce-lined serving platter.

Yield: 6 servings

Broccoli Salad

Never has broccoli been so appealing. But anything topped with bacon is a winner in my book!

2	heads (5 to 6 cups) broccoli
1	cup raisins
½	cup pecan pieces
1	small red onion, chopped
1	cup mayonnaise (more, if desired)
¼	cup sugar
2	tablespoons cider vinegar
4	bacon slices, cooked and crumbled

Wash broccoli and chop florets. Reserve stalks for another use, if desired.

Place florets in a large bowl. Add raisins, pecans, and onion.

In a separate bowl, combine mayonnaise, sugar, and vinegar. Pour mayonnaise mixture over salad and top with crumbled bacon. Stir well to coat.

Cover and chill.

Yield: 4 to 6 servings

Warm Red Cabbage with Apples

I like to serve this salad with a pork tenderloin or roast.

1	pound bacon
½	cup cranberry juice cocktail
2	teaspoons balsamic vinegar
1	teaspoon celery seed
1	teaspoon grated lemon rind
3	cups shredded red cabbage
1	large Red Delicious apple, chopped

Cook bacon in a skillet until crisp. Drain, reserving 2 teaspoons bacon drippings in skillet. Chop bacon; set aside.

Add cranberry juice, vinegar, celery seed, and lemon rind to skillet. Bring to a boil, reduce heat to low, and stir in cabbage. Cook 4 minutes or until cabbage is wilted. Add apple and reserved bacon; stir.

Serve warm.

Yield: 6 to 8 servings

Ooh-La-La French Bean-and-Bacon Salad

This is my favorite "French" dish, next to French fries with mayo!

3	slices bacon
2	cups frozen French-style green beans, thawed and drained
2	tablespoons chopped onion
2	tablespoons raisins
2	tablespoons chopped red bell pepper
¼	cup ranch dressing

Cook bacon in a skillet until crisp. Drain. Crumble bacon and set aside.

Combine green beans and next 3 ingredients, stirring well. Add dressing, stirring to coat.

Sprinkle with bacon.

Cover and chill.

Yield: 4 servings

Reduced-calorie dressing works just fine in this recipe.

Butter Bean Salad

This is one of my favorite make-ahead salads from Randy Foster, an award-winning educator and musician. He says you might want to double the recipe 'cause it'll be gone before you know it.

1	(16-ounce) package frozen shoepeg corn
2	(10-ounce) packages frozen butter beans or lima beans
1	(16-ounce) jar mayonnaise
1	bunch scallions, chopped
¼	teaspoon salt
¼	teaspoon pepper
¼	teaspoon garlic powder

Cook corn and beans according to package directions. Drain.

Combine all ingredients in a large bowl, stirring well.

Serve immediately or cover and chill overnight.

Yield: 4 to 6 servings

Greek Pasta Salad

To make this a main-dish salad, just stir in some chopped cooked chicken. I like to use deli-roasted chicken with lemon-pepper seasoning.

4	cups cooked tri-colored corkscrew pasta
1	cup sliced and chopped cucumber
½	cup (2 ounces) crumbled feta cheese
½	cup sliced black olives
½	cup thinly sliced red onion
⅔	cup Zesty Italian dressing

Combine all ingredients, tossing well to coat.

Cover and chill.

Yield: 4 servings

If I want to cut some calories, I use a reduced-calorie dressing.

Spicy Bean Salad

Be creative and serve individual portions of this salad in green bell pepper cups. All you have to do is cut the top off the pepper, remove the seeds and membranes, rinse, and drain.

1	(16-ounce) can kidney beans, rinsed and drained
1	(16-ounce) can Northern beans, rinsed and drained
1	(16-ounce) can black beans, rinsed and drained
1	(15¼-ounce) can whole-kernel corn
1	green bell pepper, chopped
1	yellow or red bell pepper, chopped
1	tomato, chopped
1	cup Italian dressing
1	teaspoon hot sauce

Combine all ingredients and stir well.

Cover and chill.

Yield: 6 to 8 servings

Star-Spangled Potato Salad

When fireworks are in the sky, the first thing I think about is a plate of barbecue and this spicy potato salad.

2	pounds small red potatoes
1	cup chopped celery
2	scallions, chopped
5	slices bacon, cooked and crumbled
1	(10-ounce) can diced tomatoes and green chilies (such as Rotel), undrained
1½	cups mayonnaise
2	tablespoons spicy brown mustard

In a large saucepan, boil potatoes until tender. Drain; cool slightly.

Cut potatoes into quarters and place in a large bowl. Add celery, scallions, and crumbled bacon to potatoes, tossing lightly.

In a separate bowl, combine tomatoes and green chilies, mayonnaise, and mustard, stirring well.

Spoon mayonnaise mixture over potatoes and toss lightly to coat. Cover and chill.

Yield: 6 to 8 servings

Peppered Black-Eyed Pea Salad

This is a great salad to take to a picnic or covered-dish supper because the longer it sits, the better it gets.

½	cup olive oil
¼	cup cider vinegar
2	tablespoons sugar
1	tablespoon minced garlic
2	tablespoons hot pepper sauce
1	teaspoon salt
2	teaspoons black pepper
1	teaspoon ground ginger
4	(16-ounce) cans black-eyed peas, rinsed and drained
1	(15-ounce) can whole young corn (sometimes called baby corn), drained
1	(2-ounce) jar pimiento, drained
⅓	cup chopped green bell pepper
1	small onion, chopped

Combine first 8 ingredients. Cover and chill for 24 hours.

Combine peas, corn, pimiento, green bell pepper, and onion in a large bowl.

Stir oil mixture well; add to pea mixture, stirring to coat.

Cover and chill.

Yield: 12 to 16 servings

Eight-Layer Salad

Everybody does a seven-layer salad—but not me. Mine is eight layers of yum!

8	slices bacon
1	head lettuce, chopped
1	cup diced green bell pepper
1	cup diced celery
1	(16-ounce) can English peas, drained
1	onion, chopped
4	hard-boiled eggs, diced
2	cups ranch dressing
1	cup (4 ounces) shredded Cheddar cheese

Cook bacon in a skillet; drain and chop.

Layer lettuce, pepper, celery, peas, onion, egg, and bacon in a trifle bowl or large glass bowl.

Spoon dressing over salad. Top with cheese.

Cover and chill at least 8 hours.

Yield: 6 to 8 servings

South-of-the-Border Salad

Sometimes I serve this salad in those refrigerated taco shells like they have at Mexican restaurants. And, of course, if you feel the need, a margarita is always a nice addition.

1	(10-ounce) package salad greens
1	(15-ounce) can whole-kernel corn, drained
1	(15-ounce) can black beans, rinsed and drained
1	cup diced tomato
2	cups (8 ounces) shredded Cheddar cheese, divided
1	cup sliced black olives, divided
½	cup ranch dressing
½	cup salsa or picante sauce
1	cup broken tortilla chips

Combine greens, corn, beans, tomato, 1 cup cheese, and ½ cup olives, tossing well.

Combine dressing and salsa. Just before serving, spoon dressing mixture onto salad.

Top with chips and remaining cheese and olives.

Yield: 6 to 8 servings

Roasted Corn-and-Gold Potato Salad

The gold potatoes in this salad are what make it special. You just can't beat the flavor combination of the buttery-tasting potatoes and the hearty roasted corn. Yum!

3	ears corn with the shucks left on, soaked in cold water
1	(5-pound) bag gold potatoes (such as Mountain King)
2	cups mayonnaise
1	cup sliced scallions
⅓	cup fresh lime juice (about 3 limes)
¼	cup grated Parmesan cheese
1	teaspoon salt
2	teaspoons Worcestershire sauce
¾	teaspoon black pepper
½	teaspoon garlic powder
½	teaspoon cayenne pepper (use more, if desired)
	Fresh chopped cilantro and chopped red bell pepper (optional)

Roast corn on the grill for 20 to 25 minutes or until corn is tender, turning occasionally. (Or roast the corn in the oven at 400°F for 20 minutes.)

Shuck corn and carefully cut kernels from cobs with a sharp knife. Set corn kernels aside. Boil unpeeled potatoes in salted water for 12 to 15 minutes or until tender but not mushy. Drain and let cool.

Place mayonnaise and next 8 ingredients in a large bowl; stir well to combine. Add potatoes and corn to mayonnaise mixture; stir well to combine.

Cover and chill. Garnish with cilantro and chopped red bell pepper, if desired.

Yield: 8 to 10 servings

Brown Rice Tabbouleh

Tabbouleh is a traditional Middle Eastern salad that's usually made with bulgur, but I think this brown rice variation is much easier. You can serve it over romaine lettuce leaves or toasted pita bread wedges.

⅔	cup uncooked brown rice
2	cups water
½	teaspoon salt
½	cup olive oil, divided
1	cup fresh lemon juice (about 8 lemons)
4	garlic cloves, minced
2	bunches fresh parsley, finely chopped
1	bunch scallions, finely chopped
¼	cup chopped fresh mint
4	tomatoes, chopped
1	cucumber, peeled and chopped
½	teaspoon salt
¼	teaspoon pepper

Cook rice in 2 cups water and ½ teaspoon salt according to package directions. When rice is done, uncover and add ¼ cup oil. Fluff gently with a fork to coat grains. Let cool. Place rice in a large bowl.

In a separate bowl, combine remaining ¼ cup olive oil, lemon juice, and garlic; drizzle over rice.

Combine parsley and next 6 ingredients. Stir parsely mixture into rice. Cover and chill at least 4 hours.

Serve over romaine leaves or warmed pita bread.

Yield: 6 servings

Ham-and-Rice Salad with Honey-Mustard Dressing

Don't get all panicked about these cute tomato cups. If you don't want to scoop out the tomatoes, just serve the salad over sliced tomatoes.

2	cups cooked long-grain rice
1	cup diced ham
½	cup chopped scallions
1	teaspoon minced garlic
1	teaspoon minced cilantro
¼	cup honey-mustard dressing (more, if desired)
3	large tomatoes

Combine first 6 ingredients and toss well.

Cut each tomato in half and scoop out pulp to form 6 cups.

Spoon rice mixture evenly into each tomato cup.

Cover and chill.

Yield: 6 servings

Macaroni Garden Salad

You can use any small-shaped pasta that you have on hand for this easy salad. If you want to get really fancy, use tri-colored pasta. If you're trying to eat healthy, use low-fat mayonnaise, light cream cheese, and whole wheat macaroni.

2	cups cooked elbow macaroni
1	cup chopped broccoli
½	cup chopped red bell pepper
¼	cup chopped scallions
¼	cup pickle relish
1	(2-ounce) jar pimiento, drained
¼	cup mayonnaise
1	(8-ounce) package cream cheese, softened
1	tablespoon mustard
½	teaspoon salt
1	cup grated Parmesan cheese

Combine first 6 ingredients, stirring well. In a separate bowl, combine mayonnaise and next 4 ingredients, stirring well.

Add mayonnaise mixture to macaroni mixture, stirring to coat.

Cover and chill.

Yield: 4 servings

Spicy Corn-and-Pasta Salad

You don't have to use pasta shells—any shape of small pasta will do.

1	(8-ounce) package small pasta shells
2	(11-ounce) cans Mexicorn, drained
1	(15-ounce) can black beans, rinsed and drained
½	cup chopped scallions
1	cup chopped tomato
½	cup orange juice
⅓	cup olive oil
¼	cup rice vinegar
1	tablespoon minced garlic
¼	teaspoon salt
3	dashes hot sauce
	Dash of pepper

For salad, cook pasta according to package directions. Drain. In a large bowl, combine pasta, corn, beans, scallions, and tomato.

For dressing, combine orange juice and next 6 ingredients, stirring well. Pour dressing mixture over pasta.

Cover and chill at least 2 hours.

Yield: 8 servings

Spaghetti Salad

Mama mia! This is some delicious salad!

1	(8-ounce) package spaghetti
1	head (about 3 cups) broccoli, chopped
5	Roma tomatoes, diced
1	cup (4 ounces) shredded Cheddar cheese
1	(2-ounce) jar pimiento, drained
1	cup Italian dressing
1	teaspoon garlic salt
½	cup sunflower seeds, toasted (optional)

Cook spaghetti according to package directions; drain and rinse in cold water. Place spaghetti in large bowl.

Trim broccoli; chop florets. (Reserve stalks for another use, if desired.)

Add broccoli, tomatoes, cheese, and pimiento to spaghetti. Add dressing and garlic salt; toss.

Cover and chill.

Sprinkle with sunflower seeds before serving, if desired.

Yield: 8 servings

And it tastes just as good with low-fat cheese and salad dressing!

Nutty Oriental Beef-Ravioli Salad

With wonderful ingredients and flavors, this is a full meal in a bowl. You can use any Oriental-style dressing you like, such as sesame.

2	(9-ounce) packages four-cheese ravioli
1	cup Oriental-style salad dressing, divided
2	cups shredded bok choy or other cabbage
¼	teaspoon salt
¼	teaspoon pepper
1	crisp red pear, sliced
1	pound deli roast beef, sliced ¼-inch thick
1	cup chopped cashews

Cook ravioli according to package directions; drain.

Combine ravioli, ½ of dressing, bok choy, salt, and pepper in a large bowl. Add pear slices and beef strips; toss.

Arrange salad on large platter. Drizzle remaining dressing over salad; sprinkle with cashews.

Yield: 6 servings

Carol's "Tuxedo" Pasta Salad

This bow tie salad is definitely not a formal affair. It's quick and easy to make and take almost anywhere. It's from my much younger and much loved sister-in-law, Carol Slaton-Bailey.

1	(8-ounce) package bow tie pasta
1	red bell pepper, chopped
1	(2¼-ounce) can sliced black olives
1	(6-ounce) jar marinated artichokes
¼	cup olive oil
3	tablespoons red wine vinegar
2	tablespoons chopped fresh parsley
2	tablespoons chopped fresh rosemary or basil
2	cups chopped cooked chicken
3	tablespoons sunflower seeds

Cook pasta according to package directions; drain.

In a large bowl, combine pasta, chopped pepper, black olives, and artichokes. Add oil, vinegar, parsley, and rosemary; toss well. Add chopped chicken; stir.

Top with sunflower seeds.

Yield: 4 servings

Festive Turkey-Pasta Salad

This is a great way to use up your leftover Thanksgiving turkey.

2	cups cooked bow tie pasta
1	cup chopped cooked turkey
½	cup chopped scallions
3	tablespoons capers
2	tablespoons dill
1	(2-ounce) jar pimiento, drained
½	cup mayonnaise
½	cup sour cream
1	tablespoon garlic salt
½	cup shredded fresh Parmesan cheese

Combine first 6 ingredients, stirring well. In a separate bowl, combine mayonnaise, sour cream, and garlic salt, stirring well.

Add mayonnaise mixture to pasta mixture, tossing to coat. Stir in Parmesan cheese.

Cover and chill at least 2 hours.

Yield: 4 servings

Hawaiian Turkey Treat

This fruit-filled pasta salad looks pretty served in a fresh pineapple shell. Stick in a little paper umbrella and make it even more festive!

3	cups cooked cheese-filled tortellini
2	cups chopped cooked turkey
1	cup diced fresh or canned pineapple tidbits, drained
½	cup raisins
½	cup coarsely chopped macadamia nuts
½	cup mayonnaise
½	cup sour cream
1	tablespoon yellow mustard
¼	teaspoon salt
¼	teaspoon pepper

Combine all ingredients, stirring well.

Cover and chill.

Yield: 4 to 6 servings

Barbecue-BLT Chicken Salad

To make this a low-fat salad, use reduced-fat mayonnaise and two bacon slices instead of four.

¼	cup mayonnaise
¼	cup barbecue sauce
1	tablespoon lemon juice
	Dash of salt
	Dash of pepper
2	cups chopped cooked chicken breast
3	cups mixed salad greens
4	bacon slices, cooked and crumbled
2	tomatoes, chopped
1	celery stalk, chopped

Combine first 5 ingredients, stirring well. Combine chicken and next 4 ingredients. Add mayonnaise mixture; toss well.

Cover and chill.

Yield: 4 servings

Leslie's Chicken Salad

This was one of our most popular salads on the menu at the Silver Spoon Café. When you're making it at home, you can stir in chopped apples or halved grapes for something different.

3   cups chopped cooked chicken

1   cup mayonnaise

½   cup chopped pecans

¼   teaspoon dried dill

¼   teaspoon garlic salt

½   cup cubed sweet pickles, drained well and patted dry

Combine all ingredients and stir well.

Cover and chill.

Yield: 4 servings

Honey-Chicken-Grape Salad

You don't have to use the roasted chicken strips—just use any kind of cooked chicken. You'll need at least 2 cups.

½	cup Catalina dressing
¼	cup honey
½	teaspoon lemon juice
1	(6-ounce) package roasted chicken strips
1	cup red grapes
1	cup purple onion slices
4	cups mixed baby greens
¼	cup sunflower seeds

Combine first 3 ingredients, stirring well. Set aside.

Combine chicken, grapes, onion slices, and greens; toss well. Drizzle dressing mixture over salad; top with sunflower seeds.

Yield: 4 servings

Cajun Chicken-Tomato Salad

If you like your chicken salad with a little "kick," this is the recipe for you! Serve it on a bed of lettuce and with hot cornbread muffins for a complete meal.

½	cup plain yogurt
1½	tablespoons lemon juice
¼	teaspoon salt
¼	teaspoon pepper
⅛	teaspoon cayenne pepper
2	garlic cloves, minced
3	cups cooked cubed chicken
3	cups diced Roma tomatoes
1	cup diced scallions
½	cup diced green bell pepper
½	cup diced celery

Combine first 6 ingredients in a small bowl; set aside.

Combine chicken and next 4 ingredients. Add yogurt mixture to chicken mixture and stir to coat.

Cover and chill.

Yield: 6 servings

Sassy Warm Shrimp Salad

Wanna show off at your next ladies luncheon? Make this and hear the applause.

2	tablespoons butter or margarine
½	cup sliced red bell pepper
½	cup sliced green bell pepper
¼	cup chopped onion
1	tablespoon minced garlic
1	teaspoon dried oregano
1	teaspoon dried basil
½	teaspoon dried thyme
½	teaspoon crushed red pepper flakes
½	cup chicken broth
1	pound large shrimp, peeled and deveined
4	cups mixed baby greens
1	cup sliced almonds, toasted

Melt butter in a large saucepan over medium-high heat. Add red bell pepper and next 7 ingredients; sauté 3 to 5 minutes until vegetables are crisp-tender.

Add chicken broth and shrimp to pan; cook 4 to 5 minutes or until shrimp are done, stirring frequently.

To serve, arrange greens on serving plates; spoon warm shrimp mixture evenly over greens. Top evenly with toasted almonds.

Yield: 4 servings

Lemon-Caper-Tuna Pasta Salad

Don't be afraid to use capers—they're not that fancy, and they add great flavor.

1	(12-ounce) package small pasta shells
½	cup olive oil
1	(6-ounce) can tuna, drained and flaked
¼	cup fresh lemon juice (about 2 lemons)
3	tablespoons capers
¼	cup caper liquid
½	teaspoon red pepper flakes
	Pinch of salt
	Pinch of pepper
1	large tomato, chopped
½	red onion, thinly sliced

Cook pasta according to directions; drain.

Transfer pasta to a large bowl; stir in olive oil. Add tuna and remaining ingredients, tossing well to coat.

Cover and chill.

Yield: 4 servings

Gazpacho

On a hot August day in Alabama, this chilled soup is just the thing to cool you down.

6	cups tomato juice
¼	cup olive oil
1	tablespoon sugar
¼	teaspoon salt
	Dash of pepper
4	tomatoes, coarsely chopped
1	onion, finely chopped
1	tablespoon finely chopped cilantro
1	cucumber, peeled and chopped
1	green bell pepper, chopped

Combine all ingredients, stirring well.

Cover and chill.

Yield: 8 servings

French Onion-Tomato Soup

Not your typical French onion soup!

8	tablespoons butter or margarine, divided
4	cups thinly sliced onion
1	garlic clove, minced
1	(46-ounce) can tomato juice
3	tablespoons lemon juice
2	tablespoons chopped parsley
2	tablespoons brown sugar
2	beef bouillon cubes
6	thick slices French bread
¾	cup shredded mozzarella cheese

Melt 2 tablespoons butter in a large saucepan. Add onions and garlic; sauté until tender. Add tomato juice and next 4 ingredients; bring to a boil. Reduce heat, cover, and simmer 10 minutes, stirring occasionally.

Spread 1 tablespoon butter on each bread slice; top each with 2 tablespoons cheese.

Just before serving, toast bread until cheese melts. Ladle soup into bowls; top each serving with French bread.

Yield: 6 servings

Broccoli Soup

Even if you think you're not a broccoli fan, you'll be lovin' it once it's mixed with enough cheese, potatoes, and beer.

3	(10-ounce) packages frozen chopped broccoli
3	(14¼-ounce) cans beef broth
1	medium onion, chopped
1	teaspoon salt
½	teaspoon pepper
1	(16-ounce) jar processed cheese (such as Cheese Whiz)
1	(12-ounce) bottle dark beer
1	cup instant mashed potatoes, uncooked
	Croutons

Combine first 5 ingredients in a Dutch oven or stock pot. Bring to a boil; reduce heat, cover, and simmer for 15 minutes.

Add cheese and beer; cook over low heat until cheese melts, stirring often. Stir in potatoes and cook 8 to 10 minutes or until thickened.

To serve, spoon soup into bowls and top each serving with croutons.

Yield: 8 to 10 servings

Nacho Potato Soup

My favorite things: potatoes, cheese, and bacon. How much better could a soup be?

1	(16-ounce) package frozen au gratin potatoes, thawed
1	(11-ounce) can whole-kernel corn, drained
1	(10-ounce) can diced tomatoes and green chilies (such as Rotel)
2	cups water
2	cups milk
2	cups cubed processed cheese (such as Velveeta)
1	cup (4 ounces) shredded Cheddar cheese
3	slices bacon, cooked and crumbled

Combine potatoes, corn, tomatoes, and water in a large saucepan. Bring to a boil, reduce heat, cover, and simmer 15 to 18 minutes or until potatoes are tender. Add milk and processed cheese.

Cover and simmer until cheese melts, stirring often.

To serve, spoon soup into bowls; top with Cheddar cheese and bacon.

Yield: 6 servings

Tortilla Soup

This is always a favorite at football parties. Serve it with plenty of tortilla chips.

2	pounds ground chuck
1	small onion, chopped
2	cups water
1	(16-ounce) can black beans, undrained
1	(16-ounce) can kidney or pinto beans, undrained
2	(11-ounce) cans niblet corn, undrained
1	(14½-ounce) can diced tomatoes, undrained
1	(10-ounce) can diced tomatoes and green chilies (such as Rotel), undrained
2	(1¼-ounce) packages taco seasoning mix
2	(1-ounce) packages ranch dressing mix
1	(8-ounce) carton sour cream
1	cup (4 ounces) shredded Cheddar or Monterey Jack cheese

Cook ground chuck and onion in a Dutch oven over medium-high heat until meat is browned, stirring to crumble meat. Drain. Return meat to pan.

Add water and next 7 ingredients to meat, stirring well. Cover and simmer over medium heat 15 minutes or until thoroughly heated.

To serve, spoon soup into bowls; top with sour cream and shredded cheese.

Yield: 8 to 10 servings

Sissy's Cheeseburger Soup

This soup is one of my precious sister Janet's recipes. She's the light of my life, the wind beneath my wings, the song in my heart, and, oh yeah, a much better cook than I am! She will always be my "Sissy." Serve this soup with cornbread to those you love!

1	pound ground beef
4	tablespoons butter or margarine
¾	cup chopped onion
1	teaspoon dried parsley
4	cups peeled, diced potato
3	(10-ounce) cans chicken broth
1	(10¾-ounce) can condensed cream of celery soup, undiluted
¼	cup all-purpose flour
1½	cups milk
8	ounces processed cheese (such as Velveeta), cubed
¾	teaspoon salt
¾	teaspoon pepper
½	cup sour cream

In a skillet, cook meat over medium-high heat, stirring to crumble. Drain and set aside.

In a 3-quart saucepan, melt butter. Add onion and parsley; sauté 10 minutes or until onion is tender. Add potato, broth, soup, and meat; bring to a boil. Reduce heat and simmer until potatoes are tender.

In a bowl, add flour to milk, stirring constantly with a whisk until flour dissolves. Add flour mixture, cheese, salt, and pepper to the soup. Cover and simmer over low heat 20 minutes or until thickened. Remove from heat; stir in sour cream.

Yield: 8 servings

Chicken-Tortilla Soup

Here's a zesty way to spice up plain canned soup.

1	(10¾-ounce) can condensed cream of chicken soup, undiluted
1	(10-ounce) can hot and spicy diced tomatoes and green chilies (such as Rotel)
3	cups water
2	cups chopped cooked chicken
4	flour tortillas, cut into thin strips

Combine soup, tomatoes and chilies, water, and chicken in a large saucepan, stirring well. Bring to a boil.

Add tortilla strips; cook over medium-high heat until mixture returns to a boil. Reduce heat to low and cook 5 minutes or until thoroughly heated.

Yield: 6 servings

Cheesy Wild Rice Soup

You'll be wild about this recipe!

1	(6-ounce) package quick-cooking long-grain wild rice mix
4	cups milk
1	(10¾-ounce) can condensed cream of potato soup, undiluted
8	ounces processed cheese (such as Velveeta), cubed
½	pound bacon, cooked and crumbled

Prepare rice in a large saucepan according to package directions. Stir in milk, soup, and cheese; cook over medium heat until cheese melts, stirring often.

Top each serving with crumbled bacon.

Yield: 6 servings

Beth's Turkey Chili

You'd be hard-pressed to find anyone who could figure out that this chili is made with ground turkey.

1	teaspoon olive oil
1	medium onion, chopped
1	tablespoon chili powder
1	teaspoon whole cumin seed
1	teaspoon ground oregano
2	garlic cloves, minced
1	pound ground turkey
1	(28-ounce) can crushed tomatoes, undrained
1	(28-ounce) can kidney beans, undrained
1	(6-ounce) can tomato paste
1	tablespoon sugar
¼	teaspoon salt
¼	teaspoon pepper
	Sour cream
	Chopped scallions
	Shredded cheese

Heat olive oil in large skillet or Dutch oven over medium-high heat. Add onion; sauté 3 to 4 minutes or until tender. Add chili powder, cumin, oregano, and garlic. Cook 2 minutes, stirring constantly.

Add turkey; cook until browned, stirring to crumble meat. Stir in tomatoes and next 5 ingredients. Cover and simmer for 20 minutes.

Serve with sour cream, scallions, and shredded cheese.

Yield: 8 servings

Of course, if you're making a low-fat chili, you probably want to use reduced-fat sour cream and cheese for the toppings.

Notes

Clockwise from top: Stir-fry Skillet Corn,
Wild Rice with Fruit and Nuts,
Spaghetti Squash Delight

Vegetables & Side Dishes

Vegetables and side dishes might be better known as "the healthy stuff that you have to serve your family along with the meat." But do not fear—I've got ways to disguise even cauliflower so that the kids will eat it!

I'm not a big veggie or salad eater. Oh, no! I would much prefer eating a box of Wheat Thins with a can of squirt cheese. But I know how important it might be to some of you dear readers to have some nice recipes that involve green or red items other than green gummy bears or red licorice sticks!

So I created some sassy vegetable dishes that I want you to try. Hey, if they're good enough for a devout junk-aholic like me, they're good enough for you and the picky eaters in your family.

By the way, in looking over these recipes, I noticed that a lot of the dishes called for cheese. Hoorah! I always hoped that cheese might count as a veggie.

Awesome Asparagus Casserole

This is a great dish to make when fresh asparagus isn't in season because it's really better to make it with canned asparagus.

2	eggs
1½	(15-ounce) cans asparagus, drained
1	(10¾-ounce) can condensed cream of mushroom soup, undiluted
1	cup crushed buttery round crackers (such as Ritz)
1	cup (4 ounces) shredded Cheddar cheese
1	cup sliced almonds
¼	cup butter or margarine, melted

Preheat oven to 350°F.

Place eggs in a saucepan and add water to cover. Bring to a rolling boil. Cover, remove from heat, and let stand 15 minutes. Drain eggs and let cool. Peel and slice eggs.

Layer asparagus, sliced eggs, crushed crackers, and soup in an 11 x 7-inch baking dish. Top with cheese and almonds. Drizzle with melted butter. Bake at 350°F for 25 minutes or until hot and bubbly.

Yield: 4 servings

Broccoli Delight

A sure way to get anyone to eat broccoli!

1½	pounds broccoli, trimmed
1	(10¾-ounce) can condensed cream of chicken soup, undiluted
½	cup sour cream
½	tablespoon all-purpose flour
2	tablespoons chopped onion
¼	teaspoon salt
⅛	teaspoon pepper
¾	cup stuffing mix

Preheat oven to 350°F.

Steam broccoli over boiling water until stems are slightly tender. Remove from heat; set aside.

Combine soup, sour cream, and flour, stirring well. Add onion, salt, and pepper.

Place broccoli in a 13 x 9-inch baking dish. Pour soup mixture over broccoli.

Sprinkle stuffing mix over broccoli. Bake, uncovered, at 350°F for 20 to 25 minutes until stuffing mix is golden brown and crisp.

Yield: 8 to 10 servings

Carrot Casserole

These carrots are so sweet and yummy, you could almost have them for dessert.

2	(16-ounce) cans carrots, drained and mashed
½	cup milk
½	cup sugar
⅓	stick butter or margarine, melted
1	teaspoon vanilla extract
2	eggs, lightly beaten
⅔	cup brown sugar, packed
⅓	cup all-purpose flour
2	tablespoons butter, chilled
⅔	cup chopped pecans
⅔	cup flaked coconut

Preheat oven to 350°F.

Combine first 6 ingredients, stirring well. Place in a 13 x 9-inch baking dish.

In a separate bowl, combine brown sugar and flour. Cut 2 tablespoons chilled butter into sugar mixture until mixture is crumbly. Stir in pecans and coconut.

Sprinkle sugar mixture over carrot mixture. Bake, uncovered, at 350°F for 20 to 25 minutes or until thoroughly heated.

Yield: 8 servings

Low-Carb Mock Mashed Potatoes

For all of you out there on a low-carb diet, here's the tasty way to replace those potatoes. Or, if you want to cut back on the fat instead, use low-fat sour cream and reduced-fat Cheddar.

1	(10-ounce) package frozen cauliflower
½	cup sour cream
½	cup (2 ounces) shredded Cheddar cheese
½	cup grated Parmesan cheese
¼	teaspoon salt
¼	teaspoon pepper
2	tablespoons butter or margarine (optional)

Cook cauliflower according to package directions and drain very well. Beat cauliflower with a mixer at high speed until smooth.

Add sour cream, Cheddar cheese, and Parmesan cheese; beat well. Stir in salt and pepper, and, if desired, butter.

Serve warm.

Yield: 3 to 4 servings

Stir-Fry Skillet Corn

This is an easy dish to whip up for weeknight suppers. Assuming, of course, that your kids will eat corn with green and red stuff in it. If not, there will just be more for the grown-ups!

1	tablespoon butter or margarine
1	red bell pepper, chopped
1	tablespoon finely chopped jalapeño pepper
1½	teaspoons ground cumin
1	(10-ounce) package frozen niblet corn, thawed
⅓	cup minced fresh parsley

Melt butter over medium-high heat in a large skillet. Add red pepper and jalapeño; sauté until tender. Add cumin; cook 30 seconds. Stir in corn and parsley. Cook 2 minutes or until thoroughly heated, stirring constantly.

Yield: 4 servings

Comfy Corn Noodles

This is a "no-brainer" side dish that's good with meatloaf or fried chicken.

1	(8-ounce) package quick-cooking noodles and butter-herb sauce mix (such as Lipton's)
1	(14¾-ounce) can cream-style corn
2	ounces processed cheese (such as Velveeta), cubed

Prepare noodles and sauce mix in a saucepan according to package directions. When noodles are tender, stir in corn and cheese; cook over medium heat 4 to 5 minutes or until cheese melts.

Yield: 3 servings

Corn Cakes with Salsa and Sour Cream

These are also good to serve as appetizers. Instead of using ¼ cup of batter for each cake, use about 2 tablespoons and make smaller cakes.

1	cup all-purpose flour
1	cup cornmeal
1	teaspoon baking powder
1	teaspoon salt
2	(3-ounce) packages cream cheese, softened
1	cup milk
1	cup butter or margarine, melted
6	eggs
1	(11-ounce) can whole-kernel corn, drained
1	cup salsa, drained
6	scallions, chopped
1	cup sour cream
	Additional salsa (optional)

Combine first 4 ingredients. Set aside.

Beat cream cheese with a mixer at medium speed until smooth. Add milk, butter, and eggs; beat well. Add flour mixture; stir just until dry ingredients are moistened. Fold in corn, salsa, and scallions.

For each corn cake, pour about ¼ cup batter onto a greased hot skillet. Cook on medium-high heat until bubbles form on top. Turn and cook until golden brown. Repeat with remaining batter.

Serve with sour cream and, if desired, additional salsa.

Yield: 12 to 16 cakes

Ratatouille-Stuffed Portobellos

Don't get all worked up about the fancy-sounding French name. Ratatouille is just an eggplant mixture with some onions, pepper, and garlic.

1	tablespoon olive oil
1	cup chopped onion
1	cup chopped green bell pepper
2	garlic cloves, minced
1	cup peeled, diced eggplant
1	cup chopped plum tomato
1	(15-ounce) can black beans, rinsed and drained
2	tablespoons tomato paste
½	teaspoon salt
¼	teaspoon ground oregano
4	large portobello mushroom caps
2	ounces shredded fresh Parmesan cheese

Preheat oven to 375°F.

Heat oil in a large skillet over medium-high heat. Add onion, bell pepper, and garlic; sauté until tender. Add eggplant and cook 2 to 3 minutes or until eggplant is slightly tender. Add tomato, beans, tomato paste, salt, and oregano, stirring well. Cook 5 to10 minutes or until mixture is slightly thickened, stirring occasionally.

Place mushroom caps in an ungreased shallow baking dish and spoon mixture into caps. Sprinkle with cheese. Bake at 375°F for 20 to 30 minutes or until mushrooms are tender.

Yield: 4 servings

Leslie's Favorite Sour Cream-Squash Casserole

This is best when you use canned squash instead of fresh or frozen.

2	(16-ounce) cans yellow squash, drained very well
1	cup sour cream
1	cup (4 ounces) shredded Cheddar cheese
1	cup grated Parmesan cheese
1	cup chopped onion
½	cup mayonnaise
1	stick butter or margarine, melted
1	sleeve round buttery crackers (such as Ritz), crushed

Preheat oven to 350°F.

Mash squash with a fork; stir in sour cream, Cheddar cheese, Parmesan cheese, onion, and mayonnaise. Place mixture in an 11 x 7-inch baking dish.

Combine melted butter and crackers. Sprinkle cracker mixture on top of squash mixture. Bake at 350°F for 30 minutes or until hot and bubbly.

Yield: 8 to 10 servings

Spaghetti Squash Delight

This "spaghetti" adds veggies to your family's diet without their even realizing it. And for all of you on low-carb diets who've given up spaghetti, this might make you feel better. Now I'll be truthful and say that spaghetti squash doesn't really taste like spaghetti (it's better!), but the strands will sort of remind you of pasta.

1	small spaghetti squash
	Cooking spray
2	tablespoons vegetable oil
1	onion, chopped
1	garlic clove, minced
1½	cups chopped tomato
¾	cup crumbled feta cheese
3	tablespoons sliced black olives
3	tablespoons chopped fresh basil

Preheat oven to 350°F.

Cut squash in half; scoop out seeds. Place cut sides down on a baking pan coated with cooking spray. Bake at 350°F for 30 minutes.

Remove squash from oven; let cool enough to be easily handled.

Meanwhile, heat oil in a large skillet over medium-high heat. Add onion and garlic; sauté until onion is tender. Add tomato and cook until thoroughly heated.

Using a fork, gently rake out strands of squash. Toss squash strands with sautéed vegetables.

Add feta cheese, olives, and basil; toss well.

Yield: 4 servings

Tasty Baked Tomatoes with a Twist

If you've got some leftover mashed potatoes, you can use them in these stuffed tomatoes. If not, take a shortcut and use frozen mashed potatoes—just make them according to the package directions. Or, try my new favorite shortcut: refrigerated mashed potatoes (such as Simply Potatoes). You don't have to do anything but open the package.

4	large firm unpeeled tomatoes
3	cups mashed potatoes
1½	cups (6 ounces) shredded Cheddar cheese, divided
½	teaspoon minced garlic
½	teaspoon salt
¼	teaspoon dried dill
¼	cup dried bread crumbs
¼	teaspoon paprika

Preheat oven to 350°F.

Cut off the tops of the tomatoes; hollow out and seed the tomatoes to form cups. Set aside.

Combine mashed potatoes, 1 cup cheese, garlic, salt, and dill. Spoon mixture evenly into tomatoes.

Combine bread crumbs, paprika, and remaining ½ cup cheese; sprinkle on top of potato mixture. Place filled tomatoes in greased muffin cups. Bake at 350°F for 10 to 15 minutes or until topping is crisp and tomatoes are thoroughly heated.

Yield: 4 servings

Tomato Pie

The pie shell to use for this recipe is one of those frozen pie shells in the aluminum pans. Don't make it hard on yourself by making your own pie crust unless you just happen to be a pastry expert.

1	(9-inch) frozen deep-dish pie shell, thawed
4	large tomatoes, sliced
8	slices bacon, cooked and crumbled
1	cup mayonnaise
1	cup shredded fresh Parmesan cheese
2	tablespoons chopped fresh basil
1	garlic clove, minced
1½	cups crushed buttery round crackers (such as Ritz)
2	tablespoons butter or margarine

Preheat oven to 350°F.

Layer tomatoes in pie shell. Top with crumbled bacon.

In a bowl, combine mayonnaise, Parmesan cheese, basil, and garlic; spread over tomatoes.

Top with crushed crackers and dot with butter. Bake at 350°F for 25 minutes or until mixture is thoroughly heated and crust is golden.

Yield: 6 servings

Autumn Root Vegetable Gratin

No, this is not a mistake—Dr Pepper really is the secret ingredient in this creamy vegetable dish. It adds the sweetness to the hearty flavors of the vegetables.

4	large baking potatoes
½	teaspoon salt
4	large turnip roots, peeled and halved
4	large carrots, grated
1	(14½-ounce) can chicken broth
1	(12-ounce) can Dr Pepper soft drink
1	cup heavy cream
½	teaspoon salt
¼	teaspoon pepper
¼	cup butter or margarine
1	cup bread crumbs

Place potatoes in a large saucepan; sprinkle with salt; add water to cover. Bring to boil and cook 12 to 15 minutes or until potatoes are tender. Drain, let cool, and cut into thin slices.

Place turnips in a large saucepan; add chicken broth and Dr Pepper. Bring to a boil; reduce heat to medium-high and cook 12 to 15 minutes or until turnips are tender. Drain, let cool, and cut into thin slices.

Preheat oven to 350°F.

Layer potatoes, carrots, and turnips in a buttered 13 x 9-inch baking dish. Pour cream over vegetables. Sprinkle with salt and pepper. Melt butter and mix with bread crumbs; sprinkle over cream. Bake at 350°F for 40 minutes or until cream is absorbed.

Let stand 10 minutes before serving.

Yield: 10 to 12 servings

Russian Potatoes

Your kids will "rush in" to gobble these down!

1	(32-ounce) package frozen hash brown potatoes
2	cups (8 ounces) shredded Cheddar cheese, divided
½	cup milk
1	(12-ounce) carton small-curd cottage cheese
1	(8-ounce) carton sour cream
1	tablespoon chopped onion
1	teaspoon salt
½	teaspoon minced garlic

Preheat oven to 325°F.

Combine potatoes, 1 cup cheese, milk, and remaining 5 ingredients in a bowl.

Spoon mixture into an 11 x 7-inch baking dish. Bake, covered, at 325°F for 35 minutes. Uncover, sprinkle with remaining 1 cup cheese, and bake 5 additional minutes or until top is bubbly and golden brown.

Yield: 4 to 6 servings

Pizza Potatoes

Because it's got sausage and pepperoni, you could even make this potato casserole the main dish. Take it to your next potluck supper instead of the usual hash-brown-and-cheese casserole.

1	pound ground sausage
½	cup pepperoni slices
1	(14-ounce) jar pizza sauce
½	cup water
1	(28-ounce) package frozen shredded potatoes
1	cup chopped onion
1	cup chopped green bell pepper
1	(2-ounce) jar pimientos, drained
1	cup (4 ounces) shredded Italian cheese blend

Cook ground sausage in a Dutch oven until browned, stirring to crumble. Drain. Add pepperoni to pan and cook over medium-high heat until thoroughly heated. Drain. Add pizza sauce and water, stirring well.

Add potatoes and next 3 ingredients. Reduce heat to medium, cover, and cook until vegetables are tender, stirring occasionally.

Sprinkle with cheese, remove from heat, and let stand until cheese melts.

Yield: 4 to 6 servings

Leslie's Decadent Mashed Potato Casserole

You'll never be satisfied with plain mashed potatoes again once you've tasted my cheesy mashed potato casserole.

4	cups cooked mashed potatoes
1	cup sour cream
½	cup chopped scallions
½	cup butter or margarine, melted
¼	teaspoon minced garlic
¼	teaspoon salt
¼	teaspoon pepper
1	cup (4 ounces) shredded Cheddar cheese
8	slices bacon, cooked and crumbled

Preheat oven to 350°F.

Combine first 7 ingredients, stirring well. Spoon into an 11 x 7-inch baking dish.

Top with Cheddar cheese and bacon. Bake at 350°F for 30 minutes or until thoroughly heated.

Yield: 6 servings

Hash Brown Potato Casserole

I love to serve this as a side dish with ham, but you can also serve it at a breakfast or brunch with sausage and eggs.

1	(32-ounce) package frozen hash brown potatoes
1	cup chopped onion
1	(8-ounce) package shredded Cheddar cheese
1	(16-ounce) carton sour cream
1	(10¾-ounce) can condensed cream of chicken soup, undiluted
1	teaspoon salt
¼	teaspoon pepper
1	stick butter or margarine, melted
1	sleeve buttery round crackers (such as Ritz), crushed

Preheat oven to 350°F.

Combine first 7 ingredients, stirring well. Spoon mixture into a greased 3-quart casserole dish.

Combine melted butter and crushed crackers. Sprinkle cracker mixture on top of potato mixture. Bake at 350°F for 1 hour or until hot and bubbly.

Yield: 8 to 10 servings

Company Sweet Potatoes

I think sweet potato casserole is a good reason to be thankful for Thanksgiving, don't you? We just can't have a holiday at our house without this casserole.

3	cups mashed cooked sweet potatoes
1	cup sugar
¼	cup milk
1	teaspoon vanilla extract
2	tablespoons grated orange rind
2	eggs, lightly beaten
⅔	cup melted butter or margarine, divided
1	cup flaked coconut
⅓	cup all-purpose flour
1	cup light brown sugar, firmly packed

Preheat oven to 375°F.

Combine first 6 ingredients and ⅓ cup melted butter, stirring well. Spoon mixture into an 11 x 7-inch baking dish.

Combine coconut, flour, brown sugar, and remaining ⅓ cup melted butter. Sprinkle on top of potatoes. Bake at 375°F for 25 to 30 minutes or until hot and bubbly.

Yield: 6 to 8 servings

You can use low-fat or skim milk in this, and it'll turn out fine.

Kim's Holiday Potato Casserole

Kim Hendrix of WSFA 12 News gave me my start on TV. She is gracious to a fault and makes a mean potato casserole.

8	medium baking potatoes, peeled and sliced
2½	teaspoons salt, divided
8	bacon slices
1	large onion, thinly sliced
⅓	cup chopped fresh chives or dill
2	cups (8 ounces) shredded Cheddar cheese
¼	teaspoon pepper
¼	cup butter or margarine
¼	cup all-purpose flour
3	cups milk

Place potatoes in a large saucepan and add water to cover. Add 2 teaspoons salt. Bring to a boil, reduce heat to medium-high, and cook 15 minutes or until potatoes are tender. Drain potatoes and set aside.

Cook bacon in a large skillet until crisp. Remove bacon and drain on paper towels, reserving 2 tablespoons bacon drippings in pan. Add onions to drippings and sauté until tender. Crumble bacon; stir bacon and chives into onion.

Preheat oven to 400°F.

Layer ⅓ of potato slices, ⅓ of onion mixture, and ⅔ cup cheese in a lightly greased 13 x 9-inch baking dish. Sprinkle with ½ teaspoon salt and ¼ teaspoon pepper. Repeat layers twice.

Melt butter in a small saucepan; whisk in flour until smooth. Gradually whisk in milk until smooth. Pour milk mixture over potato mixture; bake at 400°F for 35 minutes until golden brown and bubbly.

Yield: 8 to 10 servings

Saucy Rice

Here's a side dish that could be a one-dish meal for a weeknight supper. It'll serve 3 to 4 if it's the main dish.

1	pound ground pork sausage
1	medium onion, chopped
1	cup chopped celery
1	(28-ounce) can diced tomatoes, undrained
2½	cups water
1¼	cups uncooked long-grain rice
½	cup salsa
2	cups (8 ounces) shredded sharp Cheddar cheese

Cook sausage, onion, and celery in a skillet over medium-high heat until sausage is browned and vegetables are tender, stirring to crumble sausage. Drain.

Add tomatoes, water, rice, and salsa to pan. Cook over low heat until rice is tender.

Remove from heat; top with cheese. Cover and let stand 5 minutes or until cheese melts.

Yield: 6 servings

Green Rice

This is just about my favorite rice dish in all the world! I never get tired of making it—or eating it.

2	tablespoons vegetable oil
½	cup chopped green bell pepper
2	scallions, chopped
1	garlic clove, chopped
2	cups (8 ounces) shredded extra-sharp Cheddar cheese (such as New York State)
2	cups cooked long-grain rice
½	cup chopped fresh parsley
1	cup milk
2	eggs, lightly beaten
¼	teaspoon salt

Preheat oven to 325°F.

Heat oil in a large skillet over medium-high heat. Add bell pepper, scallions, and garlic; sauté until tender.

Combine sautéed vegetables, cheese, rice, and parsley. Stir in milk, eggs, and salt.

Spoon mixture into a 2-quart casserole dish and bake at 325°F for 40 minutes or until hot and bubbly.

Yield: 8 to 10 servings

Company Rice by Jayne

My sister-in-law, Jayne Bailey-Blake, is known far and wide for her incredible cooking skills, and this is one of the recipes she brings to our family functions. This cookbook would not be complete without her fabulous dish.

½	stick butter or margarine
1	cup uncooked converted rice (such as Uncle Ben's)
1	(10½-ounce) can French onion soup
1	(10½-ounce) can beef consommé
1	(4-ounce) can sliced mushrooms, drained

Preheat oven to 300°F.

Melt butter in an 8-inch square baking dish. Stir in rice and remaining ingredients. Cover and bake at 300°F for 45 minutes or until liquid is absorbed and rice is tender.

Yield: 4 to 6 servings

Wild Rice with Fruit & Nuts

You can start with any kind of wild rice you want to for this recipe, but my preference is quick-cooking wild rice. It tastes just the same as the kind that you have to cook for an hour.

2	tablespoons butter or margarine
¼	cup chopped scallions
¼	cup raisins
¼	cup chopped pecans
2	cups cooked wild rice

Melt butter in a large skillet over medium-high heat. Add scallions, raisins, and pecans; sauté until onions are tender. Combine raisin mixture with cooked rice; toss well.

Yield: 4 servings

South-of-the-Border Grits Casserole

We Southerners just can't make it without our grits! When we say "south of the border," we mean south of the Mason-Dixon line! This spicy grits casserole is perfect for brunches.

3	cups cooked grits
½	cup chopped onion
¼	cup butter or margarine, melted
1	(11-ounce) can Mexicorn, drained
1	(10-ounce) package frozen spinach, thawed and squeezed very dry
1	(1¼-ounce) package taco seasoning mix
2	cups (8 ounces) shredded Cheddar cheese, divided

Preheat oven to 350°F.

Combine first 6 ingredients and 1 cup cheese, stirring well. Spoon mixture into a greased 11 x 7-inch baking dish. Top with remaining 1 cup cheese. Bake at 350°F for 20 to 30 minutes or until edges are bubbly.

Yield: 4 to 6 servings

Notes

Shrimp-and-Chicken Casserole

Main-Dish Casseroles

There's an old adage that if you're a Baptist, you can't get into heaven unless you have a covered dish. Now, I'm a Baptist, so I know it's true. Just read your Bible. You know in the book of Mark where it says that Jesus took a couple of fishes and a couple of loaves of bread and fed the masses? Well, imagine what he could have done that day if he'd just had a can of cream of mushroom soup, a stick of butter, and some Ritz crackers!

I also know for a fact that there is a "Baptist Mafia." My sister Sissy is the ringleader of it at Forest Park Baptist Church in Montgomery. I'm sure that other faiths have their own version: the Presbyterian Mafia, the Jewish Mafia, the Methodist Mafia. Oh, they exist wherever two or more women are gathered in the name of feeding the sick, the infirm, or those who just need cheering up.

This chapter is dedicated to those religious Mafia princesses and the great casseroles they make. And for all of you who join me in the Church of the Profoundly Bewildered, let's just hope and pray that these other women are making enough casseroles to earn us all a spot in the heavenly kitchen.

Breakfast Casserole

Who doesn't love a breakfast casserole? I like this one because it's only got a few ingredients, and you can make it a day ahead.

3	cups stale bread cubes
1	pound ground pork sausage
2	cups (8 ounces) shredded Cheddar cheese
2	cups milk
4	eggs, lightly beaten
1	cup chopped onion

Preheat oven to 350°F.

Brown sausage in a skillet; drain.

Layer bottom of 13 x 9-inch baking dish with cubed bread. Combine sausage, cheese, and next 3 ingredients; pour over bread cubes. Cover and chill overnight.

Bake at 350°F for 45 minutes or until hot and bubbly and a knife inserted in center comes out clean.

Yield: 6 to 8 servings

Eggplant Casserole Extraordinaire

In my mind, this is the ONLY way to eat eggplant!

2	medium eggplants
2	eggs, lightly beaten
¼	teaspoon salt
¼	teaspoon pepper
2	cups bread crumbs
1	onion, chopped
2	cups (8 ounces) shredded mozzarella cheese, divided
1	(32-ounce) jar marinara sauce

Preheat oven to 350°F.

Peel and slice eggplants. Place slices in a large saucepan; add water to cover. Bring to a boil, cover, and cook 8 to 10 minutes or until eggplant is tender. Drain.

Place eggplant in a 13 x 9-inch lightly greased baking dish. Combine eggs, salt, and pepper. Pour egg mixture over eggplant slices.

Top with bread crumbs, onion, 1 cup cheese, and marinara sauce. Sprinkle with remaining 1 cup cheese. Bake at 350°F for 30 minutes or until hot and bubbly.

Yield: 6 servings

Ravioli Bake Supreme

You closet gourmets out there won't turn up your noses at this pasta dish. I think it's every bit as good as ravioli dishes I've heard about from Italy.

2	(9-ounce) packages refrigerated cheese-filled ravioli
1	(28-ounce) chunky tomato pasta sauce
1	(14-ounce) can artichoke hearts, drained and chopped
1	(4-ounce) jar whole mushrooms, drained
1	(2-ounce) can sliced ripe olives, drained
1½	cups (6 ounces) shredded mozzarella cheese

Preheat oven to 350°F.

Combine first 5 ingredients. Place mixture in an 11 x 7-inch baking dish; top with cheese.

Bake at 350°F for 30 minutes or until hot and bubbly and pasta is done.

Yield: 4 to 6 servings

Cheeseburger-and-Fries Casserole

The kids will love this one! How can you go wrong with burgers and fries?

2	pounds ground beef
1	cup chopped onion
1	(10-ounce) can condensed mushroom soup, undiluted
1	(10-ounce) can condensed Cheddar cheese soup, undiluted
1	(20-ounce) package frozen crinkle-cut French fries, thawed

Preheat oven to 350°F.

Brown ground beef and onions in a large skillet, stirring to crumble meat. Drain. Stir in soups; pour into a 13 x 9-inch baking dish.

Arrange fries on top of meat mixture. Bake, uncovered, at 350°F for 30 to 40 minutes or until fries are golden brown.

Serve with mustard and ketchup.

Yield: 6 servings

Lasagna Rollups

This low-fat pasta dish is a different twist on lasagna—instead of layering the noodles, you roll them up. It's also good made with 1 cup of thawed, drained spinach instead of the black beans.

4	lasagna noodles
½	cup (2 ounces) reduced-fat shredded Monterey Jack cheese
1	(8-ounce) carton part-skim ricotta cheese
1	(4-ounce) can chopped green chilies, drained
¼	teaspoon chili powder
⅛	teaspoon salt
1	cup canned black beans, drained
	Cooking spray
1	cup salsa

Preheat oven to 350°F.

Cook lasagna noodles according to package directions. Drain.

Combine Monterey Jack cheese and next 4 ingredients, stirring well. Spoon cheese mixture evenly over each noodle. Spoon black beans evenly over cheese mixture.

Roll up noodles, jellyroll fashion.

Place lasagna rolls, seam side down, in a square baking dish coated with cooking spray. Cover and bake at 350°F for 25 minutes or until thoroughly heated.

Spoon salsa over lasagna rolls; serve warm.

Yield: 4 servings

Tuna Fettuccine

Here's a way to dress up a plain can of tuna.

1	(9-ounce) package refrigerated fettuccine
1½	cups frozen cut green beans, thawed
2	(6-ounce) cans water-packed white tuna, drained and flaked
½	cup sliced ripe olives
½	cup creamy Caesar dressing
¼	cup half-and-half
2	tomatoes, coarsely chopped
½	cup fresh shredded Parmesan cheese

Preheat oven to 350°F.

Cook fettuccine according to package directions, adding beans when water comes to boil for pasta. Drain.

Add tuna, olives, Caesar dressing, and half-and-half to pasta mixture. Stir in tomatoes.

Place mixture in an 11 x 7-inch baking dish. Sprinkle with Parmesan cheese. Bake, uncovered, at 350°F for 28 to 30 minutes or until hot and bubbly.

Yield: 4 to 6 servings

You can use light dressing and fat-free half-and-half and it will still taste great!

Shrimp-and-Chicken Casserole

Stirring fresh shrimp into this creamy chicken dish makes it a "company worthy" casserole.

1	stick butter or margarine, divided
8	skinless, boneless chicken breasts, cut into pieces
5	tablespoons all-purpose flour
1	cup chicken broth
1	(4½-ounce) jar sliced mushrooms, drained
2	tablespoons chives
1	teaspoon lemon juice
1	teaspoon paprika
2	cups sour cream, divided
2	(10¾-ounce) cans condensed cream of shrimp soup, undiluted
1	pound fresh shrimp, peeled and deveined
¼	cup dry white wine
3	tablespoons chopped fresh parsley

Preheat oven to 350°F.

Melt ½ stick butter in a skillet over medium-high heat. Add chicken; cook 7 to 8 minutes or until lightly browned. Transfer chicken to a 2-quart casserole dish.

Melt remaining butter in a saucepan over medium heat. Stir in flour. Add broth; cook over medium heat until thickened, stirring constantly. Add mushrooms, chives, lemon juice, and paprika, stirring well. Add 1 cup sour cream; stir well. Pour sour cream-broth mixture over chicken in casserole dish.

Combine shrimp soup, remaining 1 cup sour cream, and shrimp. Pour over chicken mixture. Bake, covered, at 350°F for 1 hour. Add wine and parsley; bake, uncovered, 10 minutes.

Yield: 8 servings

Hearty Chicken Pot Pie

Instead of using a homemade pie crust, take a shortcut and use puff pastry for this chicken pot pie or split leftover biscuits.

2	(10¾-ounce) cans condensed cream of mushroom soup, undiluted
1	(10¾-ounce) can condensed cream of chicken soup, undiluted
1	(14½-ounce) can peas and carrots, drained
1	cup sour cream
1	cup (4 ounces) shredded Cheddar cheese
3	cups chopped cooked chicken breast
1	(11-ounce) can whole-kernel corn, drained
2	sheets puff pastry
1	egg, lightly beaten

Preheat oven to 350°F.

Combine first 7 ingredients, stirring well. Spoon mixture into a 13 x 9-inch baking dish.

Cut pastry sheets into hearts with a cookie cutter. Place pastry hearts on top of chicken mixture; brush with beaten egg. Bake at 350°F for 35 to 40 minutes or until crust is golden brown.

Yield: 6 servings

Enchilada Casserole

You can assemble this casserole ahead of time and then pop it in the oven when you need to serve it. The onion ring topping is my favorite part—don't bake it the whole time with them, or they'll burn.

1	(5.7-ounce) package chicken rice-and-vermicelli mix
1	(10¾-ounce) can condensed cream of chicken soup, undiluted
½	(10¾-ounce) can chicken broth
2	(4-ounce) cans chopped green chilies, drained
3	cups chopped, cooked chicken
1	cup sour cream
2	cups (8 ounces) shredded sharp Cheddar cheese
1	(2.8-ounce) can French-fried onion rings
	Paprika

Preheat oven to 350°F.

Cook rice-and-vermicelli mix according to package directions.

Combine rice and next 5 ingredients. Spoon mixture into an 11 x 7-inch baking dish; sprinkle with cheese. Bake at 350°F for 30 minutes.

Top casserole with onion rings; bake an additional 5 to 10 minutes or until onion rings are lightly browned and casserole is hot and bubbly.

Sprinkle with paprika before serving.

Yield: 4 to 6 servings

Cheddar-Chicken Spaghetti with Crumb Topping

Chicken in spaghetti? Try it, you'll like it!

1	(8-ounce) package spaghetti
2	cups cubed cooked chicken
2	cups (8 ounces) shredded Cheddar cheese, divided
1	cup milk
1	(10¾-ounce) can condensed cream of mushroom soup, undiluted
1	tablespoon diced pimiento
¼	teaspoon salt
¼	teaspoon pepper
1	stick butter or margarine, melted
2	sleeves buttery round crackers (such as Ritz), crumbled

Preheat oven to 350°F.

Cook spaghetti according to package directions; drain.

Combine chicken, 1 cup cheese, milk, soup, pimiento, salt, and pepper. Add chicken mixture to spaghetti, tossing well. Place in a 13 x 9-inch baking dish.

Combine melted butter and cracker crumbs; sprinkle on top of casserole. Bake at 350°F for 25 minutes.

Top with remaining 1 cup cheese and bake 5 minutes or until cheese melts.

Yield: 6 servings

Elegant Chicken and Rice

This is one of those great Sunday-go-to-meeting church casseroles. You'll earn a star in heaven!

2	cups chopped cooked chicken
2	cups cooked long-grain rice
1	cup (4 ounces) shredded Cheddar cheese
1	cup mayonnaise
1	(10¾-ounce) can condensed cream of mushroom soup, undiluted
1	(8-ounce) can water chestnuts, drained
1	small onion, chopped
1	stick butter or margarine, melted
1	sleeve buttery round crackers (such as Ritz), crumbled

Preheat oven to 350°F.

Combine first 7 ingredients, stirring well. Spoon into a 13 x 9-inch baking dish.

Combine melted butter and cracker crumbs; sprinkle over top of chicken mixture. Bake at 350°F for 45 minutes or until mixture is hot and bubbly.

Yield: 6 servings

Turkey Enchilada Casserole

When you just can't stand to eat another turkey sandwich, use the rest of your leftover holiday turkey for spicy enchiladas.

3	tablespoons butter or margarine
1	onion, chopped
2	cups (8 ounces) shredded Cheddar cheese, divided
2	cups chopped, cooked turkey
1	(16-ounce) carton sour cream
1	(10¾-ounce) can condensed cream of chicken soup, undiluted
1	(4-ounce) can chopped green chilies
1	cup (4 ounces) shredded mozzarella cheese
8	(6-inch) flour tortillas
1	(8-ounce) jar salsa

Preheat oven to 350°F.

Melt butter in a large skillet. Add onion and sauté until tender.

Combine onion, 1 cup Cheddar cheese, turkey, sour cream, soup, and chilies, stirring well. Spoon mixture evenly into centers of tortillas; roll up tortillas.

Place tortillas, seam side down, in a 13 x 9-inch baking dish. Sprinkle with remaining 1 cup Cheddar and mozzarella cheese. Bake at 350°F for 30 minutes or until hot and bubbly.

Spoon salsa over tortillas before serving.

Yield: 6 servings

Reuben Sandwich Casserole

If you're a fan of deli-style Reuben sandwiches, you're going to love this hearty casserole! The chopped apple adds a little sweetness to the tart sauerkraut.

	Cooking spray
6	cups cubed rye bread, divided (about 12 slices)
½	pound lean corned beef, thinly sliced and chopped
1	(16-ounce) jar sauerkraut, drained and rinsed
3	cups chopped tart apple (such as Granny Smith)
1	cup chopped onion
½	cup sour cream
½	cup prepared horseradish
1	cup (4 ounces) shredded Swiss cheese

Preheat oven to 375°F.

Place 3 cups bread cubes in an 11 x 7-inch baking dish coated with cooking spray.

In large bowl, combine corned beef and next 5 ingredients; stir well. Spoon corned beef mixture over bread cubes in baking dish, pressing lightly. Top with remaining bread cubes; sprinkle with cheese.

Bake, covered, at 375°F for 55 to 65 minutes or until apple is tender and mixture is thoroughly heated.

Yield: 4 to 6 servings

Tortilla Lasagna

The flour tortillas mimic lasagna noodles and make this easy and breezy to assemble.

1	pound ground beef
½	cup sliced green bell pepper
½	cup sliced red bell pepper
½	cup chopped onion
1	(15.5-ounce) jar cheese sauce (such as Con Queso)
4	cups (16 ounces) shredded Mexican cheese
1	(16-ounce) carton sour cream
6	flour tortillas

Preheat oven to 350°F.

Cook ground beef, pepper, and onions in a large skillet until meat is browned and vegetables are tender, stirring to crumble meat. Stir in cheese sauce.

Place 3 tortillas in a 13 x 9-inch baking dish coated with cooking spray (may have to cut tortillas to fit). Spread ½ of meat mixture over tortillas.

Sprinkle with 2 cups cheese. Top with remaining 3 tortillas and remaining meat mixture. Spoon sour cream over meat mixture; top with remaining 2 cups cheese. Bake at 350°F for 15 to 20 minutes or until mixture is hot and bubbly.

Yield: 6 to 8 servings

Pronto Pasta Carbonara

A traditional pasta carbonara has entirely too many steps and takes way too much time. I like this easy version a lot better!

3	cups uncooked penne pasta
½	cup butter or margarine
2	tablespoons minced garlic
1	(8-ounce) package cream cheese, cubed
1	cup English peas, drained
1	cup chopped red bell pepper
1	cup milk
6	bacon slices, cooked, drained, and crumbled
1	cup fresh shredded Parmesan cheese

Cook pasta according to package directions. Drain and set aside.

Melt butter in a large skillet over medium-high heat; add garlic and sauté until tender. Reduce heat to medium. Add cream cheese, peas, bell pepper, and milk; cook until cream cheese melts, stirring frequently.

Add cream cheese mixture to cooked pasta, stirring well. Sprinkle with bacon and Parmesan cheese; toss.

Serve warm.

Yield: 6 servings

Gypsy Mama's Ravioli with Sausage and Peppers

I played the role of Gypsy Mama in the Alabama Dance Theater's production of Madeline and the Gypsies. *I've hung up my tutu, but the memories will live on with this casserole.*

1   (25-ounce) package cheese-filled ravioli
2   tablespoons olive oil
8   ounces smoked sausage, sliced
2   cups frozen bell pepper and onion mix
1   (32-ounce) jar chunky pasta sauce
2   cups shredded fresh Parmesan cheese

Cook ravioli according to package directions. Drain.

Heat olive oil in a large skillet or Dutch oven over medium-high heat. Add smoked sausage and bell pepper and onion mix; stir-fry until sausage is lightly browned and vegetables are thoroughly heated.

Add ravioli and pasta sauce to sausage mixture in pan, tossing well. Cook over medium-high heat until thoroughly heated, stirring often. Sprinkle with Parmesan cheese just before serving.

Yield: 6 servings

Chili-Corndog Pie

A fair favorite made into a one-dish meal!

2	(15-ounce) cans chili with beans
6	frankfurters, cut into pieces
1	(8½-ounce) box cornbread mix (such as Jiffy)
1	cup (4 ounces) shredded Cheddar cheese
1	(4-ounce) can chopped green chilies, drained
1	egg, lightly beaten
⅓	cup milk
	Sour cream (optional)
	Chopped scallions (optional)

Preheat oven to 400°F.

Combine chili and frankfurters. Place in an 11 x 7-inch baking dish.

In a bowl, combine cornbread mix and remaining ingredients, stirring well.

Spoon batter over chili mixture. Bake at 400°F for 20 to 25 minutes or until topping is lightly browned.

Top each serving with a dollop of sour cream and chopped scallions, if desired.

Yield: 4 to 6 servings

Notes

Clockwise from top:
Dessert Pizza, Apple Shortcake with
Cinnamon Cream, Nanny's Date Balls

Desserts

I believe that there are three basic food groups: sugar, butter, and chocolate. And you'll find that most of these dessert recipes contain at least one of those vital ingredients.

The healthy types say that sugar and butter are not good for you. They'll make a lovely dessert with tofu and goat's milk and swear it tastes "just like a cream pie." But don't you believe it! According to a very wise modern writer, Fran Lebowitz, "Inhabitants of underdeveloped nations and victims of natural disasters are the only people who have ever been happy to see soybeans." Amen, sister. Amen.

I'll bet you ten bucks that this chapter will be covered with sticky fingerprints and chocolate smudges before you've even had a chance to look at the other recipes. It's a fact that in every cookbook I own, the dessert section is just about worn out.

So whether you take your sugar in a piece of cake, a slice of pie, or a morsel of candy, these no-stress sweets will give you your just desserts. Share them with others if you must.

Fried Ice Cream

How do you improve on ice cream? Fry it!

½	gallon ice cream
1	cup caramel syrup
6	cups (about 6 ounces) cornflakes
	Vegetable oil
1	(8-ounce) container frozen whipped topping, thawed
12	maraschino cherries

Place 12 scoops ice cream on a baking sheet; freeze 1 hour or until very firm.

Combine caramel syrup and cornflakes, stirring until cereal is coated (mixture will be sticky). Roll each ice cream ball in cereal mixture, coating well. Freeze coated ice cream balls again for 30 minutes or until very firm.

Fry ice cream balls in deep hot oil (375°F) for 15 to 20 seconds or until golden brown.

Drain on paper towels. To serve, place each ice cream ball in a dish and top with a dollop of whipped topping and a cherry. Serve immediately.

Yield: 12 servings

Dessert Kabobs

These kabobs look great on a dessert table, and they're fun and easy to make.

12	fresh strawberries
12	doughnut holes
6	(8-inch) wooden skewers
1	cup chocolate chips
2	tablespoons butter or margarine

Place 2 strawberries and 2 doughnut holes on each skewer.

Combine chocolate chips and butter in small saucepan. Cook over low heat until mixture is melted, stirring constantly until smooth. Drizzle chocolate sauce over kabobs.

Place kabobs on a baking sheet lined with wax paper. Cover and chill 10 minutes or until set.

Yield: 6 servings

Easter Bunny Banana Snacks

Your kids will love making these fruit treats—they're a great after-school activity and snack.

2	medium bananas
⅓	cup semisweet chocolate chips
⅓	cup Creamy Supreme milk chocolate frosting
10	pretzel sticks
	Multi-color sprinkles

Cut bananas into 10 chunks; freeze for 5 minutes or until slightly firm.

Combine chocolate chips and frosting in a small saucepan. Cook over low heat until chips melt, stirring constantly until smooth.

Insert a pretzel stick into each banana chunk. Dip banana chunks in melted chocolate; roll in sprinkles. Place coated bananas on a baking sheet lined with wax paper. Cover and freeze until firm.

Yield: 2 servings

Nutty Bananas Foster

This is a nonalcoholic version of Bananas Foster—add a splash of rum and banana liqueur if you like. And don't stress about the pound cake. Go to the bakery and buy one, or get one of those frozen pound cakes. Once you've spooned this crunchy, buttery banana mixture over it, you'll never know the difference.

½	cup butter or margarine
¾	cup dark brown sugar, packed
½	teaspoon vanilla extract
½	teaspoon ground cinnamon
⅓	cup pecan pieces
4	large bananas, sliced
8	slices pound cake

Melt butter in a medium skillet over medium heat. Add brown sugar, vanilla, and cinnamon; cook 1 minute or until sugar melts, stirring constantly.

Add pecans and bananas. Cook over low heat 3 to 4 minutes or until bananas are tender, stirring frequently.

Spoon warm mixture over pound cake slices.

Yield: 8 servings

Cherries Jubilee

Here's a show-off dessert that's so easy to make!

1	orange
1	(17-ounce) can dark sweet pitted cherries
1	tablespoon cornstarch
¼	cup orange liqueur (such as Grand Marnier)
½	gallon vanilla bean ice cream

Grate orange zest and squeeze juice from orange. Set aside.

Drain juice from cherries into a saucepan. Set cherries aside.

Stir cornstarch into cherry juice. Bring to a boil over medium-high heat, stirring constantly. Cook 1 minute or until mixture starts to thicken. Stir in orange zest and orange juice. Add cherries; cook over medium heat until thoroughly heated.

Place liqueur in a small saucepan; cook over medium-high heat until thoroughly heated. Pour over cherries; ignite.

Spoon over ice cream and serve immediately.

Yield: 6 to 8 servings

Strawberry Fool

No, I'm not referring to your husband or your ex-boyfriend. A fool is an old-fashioned English dessert made with pureed fruit and whipped cream. This easy version is for those of us who are smart enough not to spend all day in the kitchen.

1	pint strawberries, hulled
¼	cup sugar
½	(16-ounce) container frozen whipped topping, thawed
2	tablespoons chopped pecans
	Fresh strawberries (optional)

Place strawberries and sugar in a food processor; process until smooth. Fold pureed berries into whipped topping.

To serve, spoon mixture into stemmed glasses; top evenly with pecans and, if desired, additional fresh strawberries.

Yield: 4 servings

Using low-fat whipped topping helps cut down on the calories.

Crispy Dessert Balls

Try not to eat all of this yummy mixture while it's warm! It's decadent.

2	cups brown sugar, firmly packed
1	cup butter
1	(16-ounce) can flaked coconut
1	pound dates, pitted and chopped
2	cups chopped pecans
4	cups oven-toasted rice cereal (such as Rice Krispies)
	Powdered sugar

Combine brown sugar, butter, coconut, and dates in a saucepan. Cook over medium heat 6 minutes, stirring often. Remove from heat; stir in pecans and cereal.

While mixture is warm, shape into 1-inch balls and roll in powdered sugar. Let cool.

Store in an airtight container.

Yield: 3 dozen

Toffee Bars

When I'm in a time crunch, I like to make bar cookies for parties because then I don't have to spend time rolling out dough or shaping cookies. These are always a hit.

2	cups all-purpose flour
2	cups brown sugar, firmly packed, divided
3	sticks butter, divided
1	cup pecan halves
1	(6-ounce) package chocolate chips
½	cup coarsely ground pecans

Preheat oven to 350°F.

Combine flour, 1 cup brown sugar, and 1 stick butter, stirring until mixture resembles coarse meal. Press flour mixture into bottom of an ungreased 13 x 9-inch baking dish. Top with pecan halves.

Combine remaining 2 sticks butter and remaining 1 cup brown sugar in a medium saucepan. Bring to a boil and cook exactly 1 minute, stirring constantly. Pour butter mixture over pecans and crust. Bake at 350°F for 20 minutes or until surface looks bubbly. Let cool 1 minute.

Top with chocolate chips; let stand until chips melt. Spread melted chocolate with knife, covering entire surface. Sprinkle with ground pecans. Cover and chill until firm.

Let stand at room temperature before slicing into bars.

Yield: 18 bars

One-Bowl Microwave Fudge

How easy can fudge be? No candy thermometer, no saucepan, no constant stirring—just a bowl and a mixer.

1	(16-ounce) package powdered sugar
¾	cup unsweetened cocoa
1	cup chopped walnuts or pecans
2	tablespoons milk
1	stick butter or margarine, melted

Place sugar in a microwave-safe bowl. Top with cocoa, nuts, and milk. Add butter. Microwave on MEDIUM (50% power) for 1 to 3 minutes or until butter melts.

Beat with a mixer at high speed until smooth. Pour mixture into a greased 11 x 7-inch pan. Let stand until firm.

Cut into 24 squares. Store in an airtight container in the refrigerator.

Yield: 24 pieces

Orange Truffles

I love giving these at Christmas! Wrap them up in plastic wrap and pretty paper and tie the package with a fancy bow.

1	(4-ounce) package sweet baking chocolate
20	cream-filled chocolate sandwich cookies (such as Oreos), finely crushed
1	cup slivered almonds, toasted
3	tablespoons whipping cream
1	tablespoon orange liqueur or orange juice
1	tablespoon grated orange rind
1	tablespoon water
1	cup unsweetened cocoa
1	cup powdered sugar

Melt chocolate in a saucepan over low heat. Remove from heat; stir in crushed cookies, almonds, whipping cream, orange liqueur, orange rind, and water.

Cover and chill 1 hour or until mixture is cooled and firm enough to shape into balls.

Combine cocoa and powdered sugar in a shallow dish. Shape chocolate mixture into 1-inch balls. Roll balls in cocoa mixture.

Cover and chill. Store in an airtight container in the refrigerator.

Yield: 3 dozen

Milli Vanilli Chex Mix Bites

If a savory snack mix is one of your favorite holiday munchies, try this candy-coated version.

3	cups corn Chex cereal
3	cups rice Chex cereal
3	cups wheat Chex cereal
2	cups salted dry-roasted peanuts
2	cups mini-pretzel twists
2	cups mini-marshmallows
1	(20-ounce) package vanilla-flavored candy coating
1	(6-ounce) package semisweet chocolate chips

Combine first 6 ingredients in a large bowl.

Melt candy coating in a large saucepan over low heat. Stir in cereal mixture and chocolate chips. Drop mixture by spoonfuls onto wax paper.

Store in an airtight container.

Yield: 4 dozen

Creepy Crawlies

This recipe works quite well with chocolate chips too!

1	(18-ounce) package butterscotch chips
½	cup peanut butter
1	(24-ounce) can chow mein noodles
1	(6-ounce) package mini-chocolate chips

Melt butterscotch in a saucepan over low heat. Add peanut butter and cook until peanut butter melts. Stir in chow mein noodles.

Drop by spoonfuls onto wax paper. This will look like little bugs; use mini-chocolate chips for eyes.

Store in airtight container.

Yield: 2 dozen

Chocolate Delights

These no-bake treats are sure to please any crowd. All you have to do is heat up the butter-and-chocolate mixture and shape it into balls!

1	cup semisweet chocolate chips
⅓	cup butter or margarine
16	large marshmallows
2	cups quick-cooking oats
1	cup flaked coconut
½	teaspoon vanilla extract

Place chocolate chips, butter, and marshmallows in a saucepan. Cook over low heat until smooth, stirring constantly. Stir in oats, coconut, and vanilla. Let cool.

Drop mixture by teaspoonfuls onto a baking sheet lined with wax paper.

Cover and chill until set.

Yield: 2 dozen

Chocolate Bits and Pieces

If you break this into something close to 2-inch squares, you'll get about 30 pieces, but that may only be enough for two people! Watch out— they're really rich!

1	sleeve saltine crackers
1	stick butter
1	cup brown sugar, firmly packed
1	(12-ounce) package chocolate chips

Preheat oven to 350°F.

Line a jellyroll pan with wax paper or grease pan lightly. Arrange saltine crackers in one layer on pan.

Combine butter and brown sugar in a medium saucepan; bring to boil. Reduce heat and cook for 3 minutes over medium heat until butter melts, stirring constantly. Pour butter-sugar mixture over saltines and bake at 350°F for 8 to 10 minutes or until hot and bubbly.

Remove from oven; immediately sprinkle chocolate chips over the crackers. Use a spatula to spread the melting chocolate to completely cover the crackers.

Cover and chill until firm. Break into pieces.

Yield: 30 pieces

Nanny's Date Balls

This is a recipe that my mom, Bobbye Jane Middlebrooks-Morris, always used when I was growing up.

1	cup butter
1	cup sugar
1	(8-ounce) package chopped dates
1	teaspoon vanilla extract
1	cup chopped pecans
2	cups oven-toasted rice cereal (such as Rice Krispies)
	Powdered sugar

Melt butter in a medium saucepan over medium heat. Stir in sugar, dates, and vanilla. Cook over medium heat until thickened, stirring constantly. Stir in pecans and cereal.

Shape mixture into 1-inch balls.

Place powdered sugar in a plastic zip-top bag. Drop balls into bag and shake until coated.

Yield: 2 dozen

Apricot-Pecan Balls

These pretty little "bites" are perfect for tea parties.

1½	cups (about 24 cookies) crushed pecan cookies (such as Pecan Sandies)
1	cup finely chopped pecans
¾	cup sifted powdered sugar, divided
½	cup finely chopped dried apricots
¼	cup light corn syrup
2	tablespoons lemon juice

Combine crushed cookies, pecans, ½ cup powdered sugar, and apricots. Stir in corn syrup and juice.

Roll mixture into 1-inch balls. Roll balls in remaining powdered sugar.

Store in an airtight container.

Yield: 3 dozen

Cookie-Fruit Parfait

You can use any kind of cookie in this dessert, but I like it best with some kind of chocolate cookie. This is also pretty when it's layered in individual parfait glasses.

20	cream-filled chocolate sandwich cookies (such as Oreos), crumbled
1	banana, sliced
1	pint strawberries, sliced
30	seedless grapes, halved
4	(3.5-ounce) vanilla pudding cups (such as Handi-Snacks)
1	(8-ounce) container frozen whipped topping, thawed

Place ½ of crumbled cookies in bottom of an 8-inch square glass dish.

In a bowl, combine banana, strawberries, and grapes. Top cookies in dish with ½ of fruit mixture, ½ of pudding, and ½ of remaining crumbled cookies. Repeat layers.

Top with whipped topping.

Yield: 4 to 6 servings

Dessert Pizza

You can use any combination of fresh fruit or just one kind. This is a fun dessert for the kids to make and decorate.

1	(18-ounce) package refrigerated chocolate chip cookie dough
1	(8-ounce) package cream cheese, softened
½	cup powdered sugar
1	teaspoon vanilla extract
1	pint blueberries
3	kiwis, peeled and sliced
1	pint strawberries, sliced
2	peaches, peeled and sliced
2	plums, sliced
1	cup grapes, halved
1	pint whipping cream
1	(6-ounce) package white chocolate baking chips

Press cookie dough into a pizza pan. Bake cookie according to package directions. Let cool.

Combine cream cheese, powdered sugar, and vanilla; beat with a mixer until smooth. Spread cream cheese mixture over cooled cookie. Arrange fruit on top of cream cheese mixture.

Combine whipping cream and white chocolate chips in a saucepan. Cook over low heat until chips melt, stirring constantly until smooth. Drizzle over fruit.

Yield: 8 to 12 servings

Chocolate Chip Macaroons

A pretty touch is to put a chocolate kiss candy in the center of each cookie before it's completely cooled.

2	cups flaked coconut
⅔	cup semisweet mini-chocolate chips
⅔	cup sweetened condensed milk
1	teaspoon vanilla extract

Preheat oven to 350°F.

Combine all ingredients; stir well. Drop mixture by rounded teaspoonfuls 2 inches apart onto greased cookie sheets. Press gently with back of spoon to flatten. Bake at 350°F for 10 to 12 minutes or until golden brown.

Transfer cookies to wire racks and let cool completely.

Store in an airtight container.

Yield: 32 cookies

Boiled Cookies

These are better known as "cowpatties." Once you see them on the wax paper, you'll know why! But they sure are good.

2	cups sugar
½	cup milk
¼	cup unsweetened cocoa
1	stick butter or margarine
2	cups quick-cooking oats
1	cup chopped pecans
1	cup peanut butter
2	teaspoons vanilla extract

Combine sugar, milk, cocoa, and butter in a saucepan; bring mixture to a boil. Cook 1 minute, stirring frequently; remove from heat.

Stir in oats, nuts, peanut butter, and vanilla. Beat with a mixer until well blended.

Spoon by tablespoonfuls onto wax paper. Let stand 15 to 20 minutes or until firm.

Store in an airtight container.

Yield: 3 dozen

Butter Cookies

This cookie recipe came from our good friend Betty Smith. It is perfect for all occasions and very kid-friendly. You can cut the dough into moons, stars, hearts, or whatever you desire. And, you can divide the icing and add food coloring to it for more festive decorating on the cookies.

1	cup butter
½	cup sugar
1	egg
½	teaspoon almond, vanilla, or lemon extract
2½	cups self-rising flour
3	cups powdered sugar
1	tablespoon light corn syrup
2	tablespoons butter
3	tablespoons hot water

Preheat oven to 350°F.

For cookies, cream butter and sugar with a mixer until light and fluffy. Add egg and extract. Gradually add flour, stirring well.

Roll dough to ⅛-inch thickness on a lightly floured surface. Cut into desired shapes with a cookie cutter. Place cookies on ungreased baking sheets. Bake at 350°F for 8 to 10 minutes or until edges of cookies are lightly browned. Remove from baking sheets and let cool on wire racks.

For icing, combine powdered sugar, corn syrup, 2 tablespoons butter, and hot water; stir until smooth. Spread icing on cooled cookies.

Yield: 3½ dozen

Oreo Crunch Love Bars

Sometimes I think my husband "loves" these as much as he loves me!

34	cream-filled chocolate sandwich cookies (such as Oreos), divided
1	cup butter or margarine, melted
1	(7-ounce) jar marshmallow creme
1	cup semisweet chocolate chips
⅓	cup chopped walnuts

Preheat oven to 350°F.

Crumble 8 cookies; set aside.

Finely crush remaining 26 cookies. Combine crushed cookies and melted butter; press firmly into the bottom of a greased 8-inch square pan.

Dollop marshmallow creme over cookie crust to within ½ inch of edges. Sprinkle chips, nuts, and remaining crumbled cookies on top, pressing lightly into marshmallow creme.

Bake at 350°F for 8 to 12 minutes or until set. Cut into squares.

Yield: 16 squares

Portable Picnic Cookies

Keep the ants away from these sweet treats!

1	(10½-ounce) package marshmallows
1	(12-ounce) package chocolate chips
1	cup butter or margarine
3	cups oat biscuit cereal (such as Life)
1	cup peanuts

Melt marshmallows, chocolate chips, and butter in a large saucepan over low heat, stirring until smooth.

Stir in cereal and peanuts. Drop mixture by rounded teaspoonfuls onto wax paper. Let cool.

Store in an airtight container.

Yield: 2 dozen

No-Bake Coconutty Oat Cookies

The hardest part of this recipe is unwrapping the caramels!

1	cup butter or margarine
½	cup milk
1	cup sugar
1	teaspoon vanilla extract
1	teaspoon salt
25	caramel candies
3	cups quick-cooking oats
1	cup flaked coconut

Combine butter and milk in a saucepan; bring to a boil. Add sugar, vanilla, and salt; reduce heat to medium and cook 1 minute. Add caramels; stir until melted. Stir in oats and coconut.

Drop by rounded tablespoonfuls onto wax paper. Let stand until firm.

Yield: 2 dozen

No-Bake Brownie Bites

Can a cookie have too much chocolate? I don't think so.

1	(13.5-ounce) package brownie mix
⅔	cup milk
1	cup butter or margarine
1	cup creamy peanut butter
1	teaspoon vanilla extract
3	cups quick-cooking oats
1	cup candy-coated milk chocolate pieces (such as M&Ms)

Line a cookie sheet with wax paper.

Combine brownie mix, milk, and butter in a large saucepan. Bring to a boil over medium heat. Boil for 2 minutes, stirring constantly. Remove from heat.

Add peanut butter and vanilla; stir well. Stir in oats. Carefully stir in candy pieces.

Drop by teaspoonfuls onto wax paper.

Cool 5 minutes before serving.

Yield: 3 dozen

Hugs-and-Kisses Brownie Delight

This is fun to do with the kids! You might want to buy extra candies in case the kids (or the grown-ups) snack on the candy while the brownies are baking.

1	(13.5-ounce) package brownie mix
1	egg
⅓	cup oil
3	tablespoons water
1	(16-ounce) can chocolate frosting
1	(11-ounce) package almond-chocolate kiss candies (such as Hershey's Hugs and Kisses)

Prepare brownie mix in an 8-inch pan according to package directions, using egg, oil, and water. Remove from oven and let cool slightly in pan.

Spread frosting over pan of brownies. Arrange candies on top of frosting.

Cut into bars.

Yield: 20 brownies

Santa Brownies

If you want Santa to drop off plenty of gifts under your tree, leave these tasty treats out for him and the reindeer.

1	cup butter or margarine
2	cups sugar
4	eggs
6	tablespoons unsweetened cocoa
1	cup all-purpose flour
2	teaspoons vanilla extract
½	teaspoon salt
1	(7-ounce) jar marshmallow creme
1	cup creamy peanut butter
2	cups chocolate chips
3	cups oven-toasted rice cereal (such as Rice Krispies)

Preheat oven to 350°F.

Cream butter, sugar, and eggs. Stir in cocoa, flour, vanilla, and salt. Spread batter into a greased 13 x 9-inch baking pan.

Bake at 350°F for 25 minutes. Remove from oven; let cool in pan.

Spread marshmallow creme over cooled brownies.

In a small saucepan, melt peanut butter and chocolate chips over low heat, stirring constantly. Remove from heat; stir in cereal. Spread cereal mixture over marshmallow creme-topped brownies.

Cover and chill before cutting into squares.

Yield: 2 dozen

Heavenly Chocolate-Cheesecake Bars

Take these to church and you'll earn your wings for sure!

1	(8-ounce) package cream cheese, softened
1	cup sugar
1	egg, lightly beaten
1	cup chopped pecans
1	cup flaked coconut
1	(18-ounce) package refrigerated chocolate chip cookie dough

Preheat oven to 350°F.

In a medium bowl, beat cream cheese with a mixer until fluffy. Add sugar and egg; beat until smooth. Fold in pecans and coconut.

Remove ½ of cookie dough from package and press into an ungreased 8-inch square baking pan. Spread cream cheese mixture over dough. Crumble remaining cookie dough and sprinkle over cream cheese mixture.

Bake at 350°F until golden brown and firm to the touch.

Cover and chill 1 hour. Cut into bars.

Yield: 2 dozen

Mandarin Orange Cake

Buy an extra can of mandarin oranges and make a starburst on top of the cake after it's iced.

1	(18.25-ounce) package butter cake mix
4	eggs
½	cup oil
1	(11-ounce) can mandarin oranges, drained
1	(11-ounce) can crushed pineapple, drained
1	package (3.75-ounce) instant vanilla pudding mix
1	(16-ounce) container frozen whipped topping, thawed

Preheat oven to 350°F.

Combine cake mix, eggs, and oil in a large bowl, beating with a mixer until well blended. Fold in mandarin oranges. Pour batter into 3 greased and floured 8-inch cake pans. Bake at 350°F for 25 to 30 minutes or until a pick inserted in center comes out clean. Let cool completely in pans on wire racks. Remove from pans and set aside.

Place pineapple in a large bowl. Sprinkle pudding mix over pineapple. Fold in whipped topping.

Place 1 cake layer on a serving plate; spread with ⅓ of the whipped topping mixture. Top with the second cake layer. Repeat with ⅓ of the topping mixture and third cake layer. Spread remaining topping mixture over top layer.

Cover and chill.

Yield: 8 to 10 servings

Halloween Candy Pound Cake

I can't even imagine having leftover Halloween candy. At my house, if there's any candy in the bowl after the doorbell stops ringing, it's gone within the hour, especially the candy bars! But if you are the rare person who has some left, here's a great way to use it.

1	(10.75-ounce) frozen pound cake
1	stick butter, softened
2	cups powdered sugar
½	cup unsweetened cocoa
1½	cups chopped assorted candy bars

Thaw pound cake; cut into three equal horizontal layers.

Combine butter, powdered sugar, and cocoa in a large bowl. Beat with a mixer until blended. Place the bottom layer of cake on a serving plate. Spread ⅓ of frosting over bottom cake layer and sprinkle with ½ cup chopped candy.

Repeat with remaining 2 cake layers, frosting, and candy, ending with candy pieces on top.

Cover and chill.

Yield: 10 to 12 servings

Sachertorte

Make a chocolate pound cake from a cake mix or, better yet, buy one at the bakery.

1	chocolate pound cake
1	(10-ounce) jar raspberry jam
2	cups whipping cream
1	cup semisweet mini-chocolate chips
	Whipped cream (optional)
	Raspberries (optional)

Cut cake horizontally into three layers. Spread jam evenly between layers.

Combine whipping cream and chocolate in a small saucepan. Cook over low heat until chocolate melts, stirring constantly until smooth. Pour chocolate mixture over cake.

Garnish with whipped cream and raspberries, if desired.

Yield: 8 to 10 servings

Angel Food Cake with a Tunnel of Temptation

This cake is so light and delicious, you'll be tempted to eat it all at one time.

1	cup sliced almonds
2	tablespoons butter
1	(12-ounce) angel food cake
1	(32-ounce) container frozen whipped topping, thawed
1	(12-ounce) bag frozen raspberries, thawed and drained
1	(8-ounce) package cream cheese
⅓	cup chocolate topping or fudge sauce
	Red food coloring

Melt butter in a small skillet. Add almonds and sauté until lightly browned. Set aside.

Cut angel food cake in half horizontally. On bottom layer dig out a tunnel in the cake, about 1½ x 1 inch.

Combine raspberries and cream cheese, stirring well. Fold in 1 cup whipped topping; spoon into tunnel. Sprinkle sauteéd almonds on top of filling. Top with remaining layer of cake.

Add a few drops of red food coloring to remaining whipped topping; spread topping over cake.

Drizzle with chocolate sauce.

Yield: 12 servings

Apple Shortcake with Cinnamon Cream

This is a quick and easy apple version of strawberry shortcake—instead of making shortcakes, you use packaged pound cake.

1	cup brown sugar, firmly packed
1	stick butter or margarine
4	apples, sliced
1	cup pecan pieces
2	tablespoons fresh lemon juice (about 1 lemon)
1	(17-ounce) loaf pound cake
1	(8-ounce) container frozen whipped topping, thawed
	Dash of ground cinnamon

Melt butter and brown sugar in a large skillet over medium heat, stirring frequently until combined. Add apple slices; sauté until tender. Stir in pecans and lemon juice.

To serve, spoon apple mixture over cake slices; top with whipped topping and dash of cinnamon.

Yield: 8 servings

Angel S'mores Sandwiches

You'll be begging for s'more of these!

8	(1-inch) angel food cake slices
2	regular-size milk chocolate candy bars
4	large marshmallows, cut in half

Preheat oven to 350°F.

Toast angel food cake at 350°F for 5 to 8 minutes or until lightly browned.

Top each of 4 slices of warm cake with ½ chocolate bar and 2 marshmallow halves. Top with remaining cake slices.

Place cakes in oven and bake at 350°F just until chocolate melts.

Yield: 4 servings

White-and-Dark Chocolate Cheesecake
with Bourbon-Caramel Sauce

My brother, Andy Morris, is the only true gourmet in our family. Oh, sure, he grew up Southern, but now that he lives in Washington, D.C., with all the other movers and shakers, he has really come up with some fancy-schmancy recipes. He always teases our sister Janet and me about how we put cheese on everything we cook; so what recipe does he give me? Something with cream cheese! But he is adorable and one heck of a great cook. Enjoy this decadent cheesecake.

20-30	crisp sugar cookies or chocolate wafers
2½	cups sugar, divided
3	teaspoons butter, melted
4	(8-ounce) packages cream cheese, softened
½	pint sour cream
4	eggs
3	teaspoons vanilla extract
1	(10-ounce) package semisweet or dark chocolate chips
1	(10-ounce) package white chocolate chips
1	cup heavy cream, at room temperature
½	cup bourbon
1½	cups toasted whole pecans or pecan brittle

Preheat oven to 350°F.

For the crust, process cookies in a food processor until coarsely chopped. Pour crumb mixture into a small bowl; add melted butter and ¼ cup sugar. Stir until combined. Pour mixture into a 10-inch springform pan and press evenly to cover the bottom. Bake for 10 to 15 minutes or until toasted.

For the filling, process cream cheese and 1¼ cups sugar in a food processor until well blended. Add sour cream and process until smooth. With processor running, add eggs, one at a time, and process until well blended. Add vanilla and process for 30 seconds. Separate batter into 2 equal parts in 2 bowls.

In a microwave-safe bowl, heat dark chocolate chips, stirring occasionally until smooth. (Be careful not to overcook.) Add melted dark chocolate to one bowl of batter, stirring until well blended. Repeat procedure with white chocolate chips; add white chocolate to remaining bowl of batter.

Pour dark chocolate batter into the springform pan. Smooth with a spatula. Pour white chocolate mixture slowly over dark chocolate batter in a spiral motion (this will help keep the layers separate).

Bake at 350°F for 1 hour and 15 minutes or until cake is set and is slightly firm to the touch. Remove from oven; let cool 30 minutes. Run a sharp knife around the edge to free cake from the sides of the pan. Let cool 1 hour. Transfer to refrigerator and cool 8 hours or overnight.

Removed chilled cake from pan; place on a serving platter.

For the sauce, pour 1 cup sugar into a large, heavy saucepan. Cook over medium-low heat until sugar melts and turns a deep golden color. Reduce heat to low. Using a wooden spoon, slowly stir heavy cream into the melted sugar, being careful not to splash the hot sugar. The mixture will steam and bubble; use a long-handled spoon to avoid being burned by the steam. Remove from heat; stir in bourbon. Let sauce cool to room temperature.

To serve, slice cake with a sharp knife. Garnish with pecans and drizzle with sauce.

Yield: 10 to 12 servings

Pecan Tassies

No Southern cook should be without this recipe.

1	pound butter or margarine, softened
2	(3-ounce) packages cream cheese, softened
2	cups all-purpose flour
1	cup light brown sugar, firmly packed
3	tablespoons butter, melted
2	teaspoons vanilla extract
3	eggs, lightly beaten
1½	cups pecan pieces

Preheat oven to 350°F.

Combine softened butter and cream cheese; beat with a mixer until creamy. Gradually stir in flour, beating well. Shape dough into 1-inch balls and press lightly into greased mini-muffin pans to form pastry shells.

Combine brown sugar, melted butter, vanilla, and eggs; stir well. Stir in pecans.

Spoon pecan mixture into each pastry shell, filling to the top. Bake at 350°F for 25 minutes.

Remove from pans and cool completely on wire racks.

Yield: 4 dozen

Chocolate-Covered Cherry Pie

This is messy but fabulous!

1	(6-ounce) package chocolate chips
1	(14-ounce) can sweetened condensed milk
1	(21-ounce) can cherry pie filling
1	(9-inch) graham cracker crust
1	cup frozen whipped topping or whipped cream

Combine chocolate chips and sweetened condensed milk in a saucepan. Bring to a boil, stirring constantly until chocolate melts and mixture is blended. Stir in cherry pie filling.

Pour filling into pie crust. Chill.

Garnish with dollops of whipped topping or whipped cream before serving.

Yield: 8 to 10 servings

Buttered Rum-Banana Pecan Pie

You may hear an old pirate say "yo-ho-ho and yum!" when you make this decadent dish!

1	frozen (9-inch) pie crust, thawed
5	tablespoons butter, divided
1	cup chopped pecans
2	ripe bananas, sliced
20	caramel candies
3	tablespoons whipping cream
2	tablespoons dark rum
1	cup powdered sugar
1	(8-ounce) container frozen whipped topping, thawed

Bake pie crust according to package directions; let cool.

Melt 2 tablespoons butter over medium heat in large skillet. Add pecans; cook until golden, stirring often. Spoon pecans evenly over bottom of pie crust. Place banana slices over pecans.

In small saucepan, combine caramels, remaining 3 tablespoons butter, and whipping cream. Cook over medium heat until caramels melt. Stir in rum. Remove from heat and stir well. Stir in powder sugar.

Spread caramel mixture over bananas in pie shell. Let cool.

To serve, dollop each slice with whipped topping.

Yield: 8 servings

Butterscotch Dream Pie

If you want to make this a low-sugar dessert, use sugar-free butterscotch pudding mix.

2	(3.9-ounce) package instant butterscotch pudding mix
1	cup nonfat dry milk powder
2	cups water
1	graham cracker pie crust
1	cup frozen whipped topping, thawed
2	tablespoons flaked coconut
2	tablespoons chopped pecans
2	tablespoons mini-chocolate chips

Combine pudding, milk powder, and water, stirring well. Spread pudding mixture in graham cracker crust.

Spread whipped topping on top of pudding mixture. Sprinkle pie with coconut, pecans, and chocolate chips.

Cover and chill at least 1 hour.

Yield: 8 to 10 servings

Fudgy Pecan Pie

This was always popular at the frou-frou girly luncheons at my Silver Spoon Café. What is it about women and chocolate?

1	cup butter, softened
1	cup sugar
2	eggs, lightly beaten
2	tablespoons unsweetened cocoa
1	teaspoon vanilla extract
1	cup all-purpose flour
1	cup chopped pecans
1	cup chocolate chips
1	(9-ounce) frozen pie crust, thawed

Preheat oven to 325°F.

In a large bowl, beat butter and sugar with a mixer until fluffy. Add eggs, cocoa, and vanilla; beat until blended. Stir in flour, pecans, and chocolate chips.

Pour mixture into pie shell. Bake at 325°F for 30 minutes.

Yield: 8 to 10 servings

S'mores Pie

Remember those s'mores that you used to make at Girl Scout camp outs? This pie—with a graham cracker crust, chocolate, and marshmallows—will take you right back to the campfire. Oh, that we could still fit into our scout uniforms!

1	(8-ounce) package cream cheese, softened
2	cups cold milk, divided
1	(3.9-ounce) package instant chocolate pudding mix
1	cup chocolate chips
½	cup mini-marshmallows
1	(9-inch) graham cracker crust

Combine cream cheese and ½ cup milk in a medium bowl; beat with a mixer until smooth. Add pudding mix and remaining milk, beat until blended. Fold in chocolate chips and marshmallows. Pour into crust.

Cover and chill.

Yield: 8 to 10 servings

Valentine Sweetheart Pie

If you make this for your sweetie, I guarantee that you'll get a big ol' kiss!

1	cup crushed pretzels
1	cup sugar
1	cup butter, melted
1	(14-ounce) can sweetened condensed milk
1	cup frozen concentrated margarita mix, thawed
1	(10-ounce) package frozen strawberries in syrup, thawed
1	cup frozen whipped topping, thawed
	Sliced strawberries (optional)

Combine first 3 ingredients in a small bowl, stirring well. Press mixture firmly into bottom of an ungreased 9-inch springform pan. Cover and chill.

Combine condensed milk and margarita mix in a large bowl. Beat with a mixer at medium speed until smooth. Add strawberries; beat at low speed until well blended. Fold in whipped topping.

Spoon mixture into prepared crust. Cover and freeze 3 hours or until firm.

Garnish with additional sliced strawberries, if desired.

Yield: 8 to 12 servings

Whipped Kahlúa Pie

I love a strong cup of coffee with this dessert.

2	cups frozen whipped topping, thawed
⅓	cup Kahlúa
4	regular-size Heath candy bars, crushed
1	quart coffee ice cream, softened
1	(9-inch) chocolate pie crust

Fold whipped topping, Kahlúa, and 3 crushed candy bars into ice cream.

Spoon mixture into pie crust. Sprinkle with remaining crushed candy bar.

Cover and freeze.

Yield: 8 servings

Peanut Butter Pie

"You got peanut butter in my chocolate!" "You got chocolate in my peanut butter!" It doesn't matter how the peanut butter and chocolate got together—you'll love this pie!

1	(8-ounce) package cream cheese, softened
1	cup creamy peanut butter
1	cup powdered sugar
1	(8-ounce) container frozen whipped topping, thawed
12	mini-peanut butter-chocolate cups (such as Reese's Cups), chopped
1	(9-inch) chocolate pie crust

Combine cream cheese, peanut butter, and powdered sugar, stirring until smooth. Fold in ½ of whipped topping and ½ of the chopped candy pieces.

Spoon mixture into pie crust.

Top with remaining whipped topping and sprinkle with remaining candy pieces.

Yield: 8 servings

Pineapple-Sour Cream Pie

A tropical delight!

1	(9-inch) frozen pie crust, thawed
2	(8-ounce) cans crushed pineapple
1	(3.75-ounce) package instant vanilla pudding mix
1	tablespoon sugar
1	(8-ounce) carton sour cream
1	(8-ounce) container frozen whipped topping, thawed

Prebake pie crust according to package directions. Let cool.

Drain 1 can pineapple, reserving juice for another use. Combine 1 can drained pineapple, 1 undrained can pineapple, pudding mix, and next 3 ingredients in a large bowl; stir well to blend (do not use a mixer).

Spoon filling into crust. Cover and chill 2 to 3 hours or until set.

Yield: 6 to 8 servings

Mrs. Turner's Coconut Dream Pie

This recipe is from one of my church buddies. She was an angel to share it with me.

1	(9-inch) frozen pie crust, thawed
1	(8-ounce) package cream cheese, softened
1	(14-ounce) can sweetened condensed milk
1	(8-ounce) container frozen whipped topping, thawed
1	stick butter
1	cup pecan pieces
1	cup flaked coconut

Bake pie crust according to package directions. Let cool.

Beat cream cheese, milk, and whipped topping with a mixer until smooth. Cover and chill.

Melt butter in a skillet over medium heat. Add pecans and coconut. Cook over medium heat until browned, stirring frequently.

Spoon ½ of coconut mixture into baked pie crust. Top with cream cheese mixture. Cover and chill.

Top with remaining coconut mixture before serving.

Yield: 6 to 8 servings

Toffee-Mocha Trifle

This looks beautiful on a dessert buffet. It can be your secret if you use low-fat ingredients!

1	(12-ounce) angel food cake, cut into cubes
1	cup strong brewed coffee, cooled
1	(8-ounce) package cream cheese, softened
¾	cup chocolate syrup
3	tablespoons sugar
2	cups frozen whipped topping, thawed
3	regular-size Heath candy bars, crushed

Place cake cubes in a large bowl. Drizzle with coffee and toss lightly. Set aside.

In a separate bowl, combine cream cheese, chocolate syrup, and sugar; stir until well blended. Fold in whipped topping.

Place ⅓ of cake cubes in a trifle dish or straight-sided glass bowl. Spoon ⅓ of cream cheese mixture over cake cube layer. Repeat layers twice; top with crushed candy bars.

Cover and chill at least 1 hour before serving.

Yield: 10 servings

Leslie's Super-Easy Valentine Trifle

If you or your Valentine sweetie needs to lose a few pounds, you can make this a low-fat treat: follow the low-fat directions on the brownie mix package and use fat-free pudding cups and fat-free frozen whipped topping.

1	(13.5-ounce) package brownie mix
1	egg
⅓	cup vegetable oil
6	(3.5-ounce) containers chocolate pudding
1	(8-ounce) container frozen whipped topping, thawed
2	pints strawberries, hulled and sliced
6	heart-shaped sugar cookies from the bakery (optional)

Prepare brownies according to package directions, using egg and oil. Bake according to package directions in an 8-inch square pan. Let cool.

If desired, stand heart shaped cookies around the edge of bowl before layering in the brownies, pudding, and berries.

Crumble ½ of the brownies in the bottom of a trifle bowl or large glass bowl.

Combine chocolate pudding and whipped topping, stirring well. Spoon ½ of pudding mixture over crumbled brownie layer; top with ½ of the strawberries. Repeat layers with remaining brownies, pudding, and strawberries.

Yield: 8 to 10 servings

Blueberry-Lemon Trifle

If you can't find an angel food cake in the grocery store bakery, use a bakery pound cake.

3	cups fresh blueberries, divided
2	(15-ounce) cans lemon pie filling
2	(8-ounce) cartons lemon or vanilla yogurt
1	(12-ounce) angel food cake, cut into 1-inch cubes
2	cups whipped cream
12	lemon slices (about 2 lemons), seeds removed

Set aside ⅓ cup of blueberries for garnish.

Combine yogurt and lemon pie filling, stirring well.

Place ⅓ of cake cubes in a trifle dish or other straight-sided glass bowl. Top with ⅓ of lemon pie filling mixture and ⅓ of blueberries.

Repeat layers twice. Top with whipped cream. Garnish with blueberries and lemon slices.

Yield: 6 to 8 servings

Bread Pudding with Bourbon Sauce

Very basic. Very easy. Very good.

12	slices bread
½	cup raisins
2	(14-ounce) cans sweetened condensed milk
4	eggs, lightly beaten
3	teaspoons vanilla extract, divided
½	teaspoon ground cinnamon
½	cup butter or margarine
¼	cup bourbon

Preheat oven to 350°F.

For pudding, tear bread into pieces; place in lightly greased 8-inch square pan. Sprinkle raisins over bread.

In a bowl, combine 1 can condensed milk, eggs, 2 teaspoons vanilla, and cinnamon, stirring well. Pour milk mixture over bread and raisins.

Place pan in a large, shallow roasting pan. Add hot water to a depth of 1 inch. Bake at 350°F for 35 to 40 minutes or until set.

For sauce, combine remaining can condensed milk and butter in a medium saucepan. Cook over low heat until butter melts, stirring frequently. Remove from heat; stir in bourbon and remaining 1 teaspoon vanilla.

Serve pudding warm with warm bourbon sauce.

Yield: 10 servings

Sweet Kugel

This sweet noodle casserole is a traditional Jewish dish often served on the Sabbath. It can be either a dessert or a sweet side dish. I vote for having it as a side dish so that we can still have dessert!

1	(16-ounce) package wide egg noodles
2	sticks butter, divided
1	cup pecan halves
1	cup light brown sugar, firmly packed
⅔	cup sugar
3	eggs, lightly beaten
1	teaspoon salt
1	teaspoon ground cinnamon
	Fresh fruit, such as berries, grapes, or sliced oranges (optional)

Preheat oven to 350°F.

Cook noodles according to package directions. Drain.

Melt 1 stick of butter in a saucepan. Add pecans and brown sugar to melted butter, stirring well. Pour pecan mixture into bottom of a Bundt pan.

Melt remaining stick of butter; combine cooked noodles, sugar, eggs, salt, and cinnamon. Pour into Bundt pan over pecan mixture. Bake, covered, at 350°F for 1 hour. Uncover and bake 5 additional minutes.

Invert on platter; garnish with fresh fruit.

Yield: 6 servings

Oreo Pancakes

If you're like me and think that no meal is complete without dessert, why not just make dessert your breakfast?

1	cup milk
1	egg, lightly beaten
2	tablespoons vegetable oil
1	cup baking mix (such as Bisquick)
1	cup (about 12 cookies) crumbled cream-filled chocolate sandwich cookies (such as Oreos)
2	bananas, sliced
1	cup strawberries, sliced
1	cup frozen whipped topping, thawed
	Pancake syrup

Combine milk, egg, and oil, stirring well. Add baking mix, stirring just until mix is moistened. Stir in 1 cup crumbled cookies.

For each pancake, pour about ¼ cup batter onto a hot, lightly greased griddle or skillet. Cook pancakes until tops are covered with bubbles and edges look cooked. Turn and cook other side. Repeat with remaining batter.

Top pancakes with bananas, strawberries, whipped topping, and syrup.

Yield: 6 to 8 pancakes

If your conscience bothers you, you can use low-fat or skim milk and low-fat whipped topping.

Marshmallow Puffs

As if marshmallows could get any better!

	Cooking spray
1	cup sugar
2	tablespoons all-purpose flour
1	teaspoon ground cinnamon
2	(8-ounce) cans refrigerated crescent dinner rolls
16	large marshmallows
1	cup butter or margarine, melted
1	cup powdered sugar
1	teaspoon vanilla extract
2	teaspoons milk (add a little more, if desired)
½	cup chopped almonds

Preheat oven to 350°F.

Coat 16 muffin cups with cooking spray.

For puffs, combine sugar, flour, and cinnamon in a shallow bowl. Separate dinner roll dough into 16 triangles.

Dip marshmallows in melted butter; roll in sugar mixture. Wrap a dough triangle around each marshmallow, completely covering marshmallow. Brush with melted butter and bake at 350°F for 12 to 15 minutes or until lightly browned.

For glaze, combine powdered sugar, vanilla, and milk, stirring until blended. Drizzle glaze over rolls; top with chopped almonds.

Yield: 16 servings

Producing this book has been a labor of love for many generous people.

Thanks to my wonderful husband, Paul Bailey, Jr. He certainly deserves a medal for putting up with me (and our cat children, Bunny, Spooky, and Pooter) for almost fifteen years. He is the love of my life, and he keeps me full of joy. My sweet Paul also taught me just how great a "three-bass day" can be!

To my baby sister, Janet, and my baby brother, Andy (okay, so they are in their 40s; they will always be the babies to me). Thanks for making us the three amigos, three peas in a pod, the three stooges. I love you. (And yes, they are much better cooks than I am.)

To my special friend, Thomas Cornacchia, I'm glad you're a part of the family, and peace to you.

To Carolyn and Dr. Al Newman, who have always believed in me, I hope to make you proud. (A special thank-you to Dr. Al for getting rid of the kidney stones during the writing of this book. Ow!)

To the incredible staff of River City Publishing: Lissa, Ashley, Gail, William, Chappell, and Travis.

To my staff at Silver Spoon a la Carte Café and Catering, you fed my soul and my tummy.

To anchor Kim Hendrix and producer Carrie Gerber of WSFA 12, who made me a "star" on TV, you are like sisters to me.

To WSFA 12's Michael Briddell and Rich Thomas, who will eat anything I cook.

To incredibly talented photographer Russ Baxley for fabulous interior and cover shots for the book. To Ms. Lewis Ann Harris, my food stylist, who is truly the real talent in my kitchen. And because I'm a high-maintenance kind of girl, special thanks to Eduardo Pajaro Guardo for makeup and hair for the book cover (he worked miracles).

To Anne Cain, who edited this book with a fine-tooth comb and never complained about how late I was in getting all the recipes to her!

Special thanks to Larry Stevens and Rusty Aldridge, my radio cohorts in crime, who kept me laughing even when I wanted to cry.

To my precious in-laws, Betty and P.B., who treat me like I'm really their daughter.

To Carol, Clay, Jayne, James, and all my nieces and nephews, thank you for showing me what family is all about.

To my brother-in-law, Sonny Wheat, thanks for loving my sister Janet and putting up with me!

A kiss goes out to a very special Aunt Hazel, whose banana pudding makes you want to "slap yo' mama"!

Lastly, thanks to my dad, Bill Morris; my mom, Bobby Jane Morris; and my older sister, Kathy Morris, who I feel watching me from Heaven. I hope you know how much you are missed.

Recipe Index